FREE DVD   FREE DVD

From Stress to Success DVD from Trivium Test Prep

Dear Customer,

Thank you for purchasing from Trivium Test Prep! Whether you're looking to join the military, get into college, or advance your career, we're honored to be a part of your journey.

To show our appreciation (and to help you relieve a little of that test-prep stress), we're offering a **FREE *ASVAB Essential Test Tips DVD*** by Trivium Test Prep. Our DVD includes 35 test preparation strategies that will help keep you calm and collected before and during your big exam. All we ask is that you email us your feedback and describe your experience with our product. Amazing, awful, or just so-so: we want to hear what you have to say!

To receive your **FREE *ASVAB Essential Test Tips DVD***, please email us at 5star@triviumtestprep.com. Include "Free 5 Star" in the subject line and the following information in your email:

1. The title of the product you purchased.
2. Your rating from 1–5 (with 5 being the best).
3. Your feedback about the product, including how our materials helped you meet your goals and ways in which we can improve our products.
4. Your full name and shipping address so we can send your **FREE *ASVAB Essential Test Tips DVD***.

If you have any questions or concerns please feel free to contact us directly at 5star@triviumtestprep.com.

Thank you, and good luck with your studies!

ASVAB Practice Test Book 2022-2023:

Exam Prep with 450 Questions and Detailed Answers

Elissa Simon

Copyright © 2022 by Trivium Test Prep

ISBN-13: 9781637981986

ALL RIGHTS RESERVED. By purchase of this book, you have been licensed one copy for personal use only. No part of this work may be reproduced, redistributed, or used in any form or by any means without prior written permission of the publisher and copyright owner. Trivium Test Prep; Accepted, Inc.; Cirrus Test Prep; and Ascencia Test Prep are all imprints of Trivium Test Prep, LLC.

USAF was not involved in the creation or production of this product, is not in any way affiliated with Trivium Test Prep, and does not sponsor or endorse this product. All test names (and their acronyms) are trademarks of their respective owners. This study guide is for general information and does not claim endorsement by any third party.

Image(s) used under license from Shutterstock.com

TABLE OF CONTENTS

INTRODUCTION		i
1 PRACTICE TEST ONE		**1**
	General Science	1
	Arithmetic Reasoning	4
	Word Knowledge	8
	Paragraph Comprehension	11
	Math Knowledge	16
	Electronics	19
	Automotive and Shop Information	22
	Mechanical Comprehension	25
	Assembling Objects	29
	Answer Key	43

2 PRACTICE TEST TWO		**69**
	General Science	69
	Arithmetic Reasoning	72
	Word Knowledge	76
	Paragraph Comprehension	79
	Math Knowledge	85
	Electronics	88
	Automotive and Shop Information	91
	Mechanical Comprehension	94
	Assembling Objects	97
	Answer Key	111

INTRODUCTION

Congratulations on choosing to take the Armed Services Vocational Aptitude Battery (ASVAB) exam! By purchasing this book, you've taken an important step on your path to joining the military.

This guide will provide you with a detailed overview of the ASVAB, so you know exactly what to expect on exam day. We'll take you through all the concepts covered on the exam and give you the opportunity to test your knowledge with practice questions. Even if it's been a while since you last took a major exam, don't worry; we'll make sure you're more than ready!

What Is the ASVAB?

The ASVAB exam is designed to assess the aptitude of individuals aspiring to gain entrance into any of the five branches of the US Armed Forces. All applicants must pass the ASVAB as one of the qualifications to join the military. The ASVAB testing program is under the purview of the Department of Defense and is administered at regional Military Entrance Processing Stations (MEPS) or local satellite offices called Military Entrance Test (MET) sites. Military personnel administer the exam at MEPS locations, while typically civilian contractors or government employees administer the exam at the MET sites.

High school students in grades 11 and 12 are eligible to take the exam as well as students in postsecondary schools. In order for your exam score to be considered for enlistment, you must have attained the age of seventeen when you take the oath to join the military, and your exam score must be no more than two years old. Adults who wish to take the ASVAB and join the military must be no older than the maximum age accepted by their desired branch of service at the time of enlistment.

There are two versions of the ASVAB applicants may take—the computerized (CAT-ASVAB) and the paper-and-pencil ASVAB exam. Please note that current military members who wish to increase their score to qualify for certain advanced schooling should take the Armed Forces Classification Exam (AFCT).

Computer Adaptive Testing

Computer adaptive testing (CAT) allows the test administrators to get a more complete view of your skills in less time and with fewer questions. These tests start with a question of average difficulty. If you answer this question correctly, the next question will be harder; if you answer it incorrectly, the next question will be easier. This continues as you go through the section, with questions getting harder or easier based on how well you perform. Once you've answered enough questions for the computer to determine your score, that section of the test will end.

Often you will be able to immediately see your score after taking a CAT exam. You will also probably answer fewer questions than if you'd taken a paper-and-pencil test, and the section will take less time. However, you will not be able to go back and check or change your answers.

The ASVAB is offered in both CAT and paper-and-pencil form. The paper-and-pencil ASVAB exams are typically administered at MET sites where the CAT-ASVAB exam computer stations or military testing personnel are not available, such as high schools or at the National Guard Armory.

Retaking the ASVAB

If you are not satisfied with your ASVAB score, you may retake the ASVAB exam. The first two retake exams must be completed at least one calendar month from the date of the initial exam. After the second retake, applicants must wait at least six calendar months to retake the exam. ASVAB exam results are valid for two years.

WHAT'S ON THE ASVAB?

The ASVAB consists of ten subtests. In the following table, each subtest is listed with the approximate number of questions and the time limit allowed. Once you finish a subtest (or time runs out), you cannot return to that section. All questions are in a multiple-choice format. Applicants use the computer keyboard and mouse to select answers for the CAT-ASVAB and bubble answer sheets to select answers for the paper-and-pencil ASVAB.

What's on the ASVAB?

Subject	CAT-ASVAB		PAPER-AND-PENCIL ASVAB	
	Approximate Number of Questions	Time Limit	Approximate Number of Questions	Time Limit
General Science	16	8 minutes	25	11 minutes
Arithmetic Reasoning	16	39 minutes	30	36 minutes
Word Knowledge	16	8 minutes	35	11 minutes
Paragraph Comprehension	11	22 minutes	15	13 minutes
Mathematics Knowledge	16	20 minutes	25	24 minutes
Electronics	16	8 minutes	20	9 minutes
Auto Information	11	7 minutes	25	11 minutes
Shop Information	11	6 minutes	This subtest is combined with the Auto Information subtest.	
Mechanical Comprehension	16	20 minutes	25	19 minutes
Assembling Objects	16	16 minutes	25	15 minutes
Total	145 questions	2 hours, 34 minutes	225 questions	2 hours, 29 minutes

Breakdown of the Subtests

General Science (GS): tests your knowledge and application of Earth and physical sciences, biology, chemistry, and physics.

Arithmetic Reasoning (AR)*: tests your ability to calculate mathematical word problems using basic addition, subtraction, multiplication, division, percentages, ratio, and proportions.

Word Knowledge (WK)*: identifies the breadth of your vocabulary by asking you to select the correct meaning of a word, synonyms, and antonyms.

Paragraph Comprehension (PC)*: tests your reading comprehension through analysis of reading passages.

Mathematics Knowledge (MK)*: asks you to solve secondary-level math problems involving algebra, geometry, and converting fractions.

Electronics Information (EI): tests your ability to employ electrical circuits and formulas, identify their components, and use terminology.

Auto Information (AI)**: tests your knowledge of vehicle systems (e.g., engines, transmissions, and brakes) and repair techniques.

Shop Information (SI)**: tests your knowledge of correct tool use, shop terminology, and wood and metal shop practices.

Mechanical Comprehension (MC): asks you about basic mechanical principles surrounding levers and pulleys, complex machinery, force, mass, and kinetic energy.

Assembling Objects (AO): tests your spatial orientation skills by asking you to identify how objects fit together.

*Indicates the subtests used to compose the AFQT score.

**For the paper-and-pencil ASVAB exam, the Auto Information and Shop Information subtests are combined into one subtest. The score received for this subtest is listed as AS.

HOW IS THE ASVAB SCORED?

The ASVAB Score

Raw scores (number of correct answers) from four of the ten ASVAB subtests (Word Knowledge [WK], Paragraph Comprehension [PC], Arithmetic Reasoning [AR], and Mathematic Knowledge [MK]) are computed and weighted to make up the Armed Forces Qualification Exam (AFQT) score.

To calculate the AFQT score, the WK and PC scores are added together and compared to a Verbal Expression chart to get the Verbal Expression (VE) value. This new VE value is doubled. Add to the VE value the MK and AR weighted scores to get the overall AFQT score.

For example, suppose you received the following points for each of the categories:
- WK—15; PC—11; MK—32; AR—42
- Add 15 + 11 = 26. The score 26 equates to 40 for a VE value.
- Double the VE value = 80.
- Add 80 + 32 + 42 = 154.
- The total of 154 equates to 38 as an AFQT score.

Please note that the MK and AR raw scores are not used in computing the overall AFQT score. Applicants receive additional points for correctly answering more difficult questions in these two subtests, thus resulting in a weighted score.

The Standard Score

The Standard Score compares your raw scores (number of correct answers) combining the WK, PC, AR, and MK subtests to those of other applicants between the ages of eighteen and twenty-three. It is displayed as a percentile ranking (1–99 percent).

The Service Composite Score

Together with their recruiter, applicants may select a certain career field or military occupational specialty (MOS) depending on their ASVAB score. This score not only determines eligibility for entry into the military; it is also an indicator of which career field would best suit the individual. The score you receive may qualify or disqualify you for certain MOS within your chosen career field. Selection for assignment to some MOS requires higher scores than others. This is important to know if you wish to enter into a technical MOS. Ask your recruiter for qualifying scores of MOS that you may be interested in pursuing.

The Service Composite Score is the score the services use to determine if an applicant meets the qualifications for a specific MOS. The US Army, Air Force, and Marine Corps determine the Service Composite Score by calculating the raw scores from a combination of ALL subtests, not just the four subtests making up the AFQT score. These scores are known as line (or composite) scores. The Air Force uses the Numerical Operations (NO) and Coding Speed (CS) line scores in addition to the Standard Scores. Examples of the line (composite) scores needed for certain MOSs are as follows:

- Army AVENGER System repairer job: Add GS + AS + MK + EI. The total score must be 98 or above.
- Air Force in-flight refueler job: Add AR + VE. The total score must be 53 or above.
- Marine intelligence specialist job: Add VE + AR. The total score must be 100 or above.
- Navy aviation boatswain mate job: Add VE + AR + MK + AS. The total score must be 184 or above.
- Coast Guard: Add VE +AR. The total score must be 109 or above.

The Career Exploration Score

The Career Exploration Program is a tool for recruiters to identify aptitude and career interest in high school and postsecondary students. Students take the ASVAB and combine it with an interest inventory. Together these documents and results help pave the path for students with an interest in joining the military. This program is marketed specifically in select high schools and colleges. Students interested in this program should contact their local recruiter or high school counselor.

Qualifying Scores

Being fully qualified for military service requires applicants to achieve many benchmarks. To qualify for military service, applicants who possess a high school diploma must achieve different scores on the ASVAB than applicants with a General Education Development (GED). The Department of Defense places applicants in one of three tiers.

- Tier 1 applicants possess a high school diploma or some college.
- Tier 2 applicants possess a GED.

- Tier 3 applicants do not possess an educational certificate or diploma.

Tier 3 applicants must score higher on the AFQT than a Tier 2 applicant. Likewise, a Tier 2 applicant must score higher on the AFQT than a Tier 1 applicant.

Recruitment goals always change, so an applicant who is Tier 3 may not qualify at all despite the AFQT score. Contact your recruiter for eligibility requirements.

Additionally, one qualifying score for the Army may not qualify that same individual for the Air Force.

The minimum ASVAB scores required for each service for applicants with at least a high school diploma or GED are as follows:
- US Air Force—36 with a diploma; 65 with a GED
- US Army—31 with a diploma; 50 with a GED
- Coast Guard—40 with a diploma; 50 with a GED
- Marine Corps—32 with a diploma; 50 with a GED
- National Guard—31 with a diploma; 50 with a GED
- US Navy—35 with a diploma; 50 with a GED

How Is the ASVAB Administered?

If you are ready to take the ASVAB, contact your local recruiter. Your recruiter will determine your initial qualifications and schedule you for the ASVAB. The location where you take the ASVAB will decide when a test seat is available.

On the day of the exam, you will need to bring valid photo identification to verify your identity. Testing materials are provided by the test proctor. Calculators are not allowed. If your recruiter drives you to the testing location, the recruiter cannot be in the testing room. Personal breaks are scheduled by the proctor, so be prepared to remain in the testing seat until dismissed.

Getting to Know the United States Military

Joining the greatest and strongest military force in the world is an honor for which only a few qualify. If you have not decided on a specific branch of service, research all branches, as they offer a wide array of careers to choose from. Each branch of service has unique missions that it is commonly known for; for instance, the Army is known for land mission operations, Air Force is primarily jet aviation, Navy for sea operations, Coast Guard for sea border patrolling, and the Marines for worldwide security. To support these unique missions, all branches share certain identical career fields (e.g., administrative, pilots, and maintenance specialists) to choose from.

The rank structure of the military branches is broken down into three categories: enlisted, warrant officers, and commissioned officers. Enlisted members may join straight out of high school, and the military provides job training after basic training. Warrant officers are current military members who apply and qualify for advanced specialized training in certain technical career fields. They are considered technical experts in their career fields. As warrant officers, they are saluted by enlisted personnel. Commissioned officers enter the service after earning a four-year college degree or successful completion at a military academy or Reserve Officer Training Corp (ROTC) program. Commissioned officers are trained in tactics and leadership courses to lead the enlisted members assigned to them.

The Military Recruitment Process

As stated before, passing the ASVAB is just one requirement for military service qualification. You may contact your local recruiter through your high school counselor or college adviser, or visit your local military recruitment center.

Once you contact your local recruiter, he or she will meet with you at the recruiting office, your school, or your home. During this meeting, the recruiter will conduct an interview to initiate the recruitment process. This process begins with the recruiter determining if you meet the basic qualification requirements. Expect a review of your education level, financial record, background investigation, interests, criminal record or drug history, height and weight, age, and citizenship. Once basic qualifications have been established, the recruiter schedules you to take the ASVAB exam and a physical exam. After these, you will meet with your recruiter to discuss your ASVAB scores and any medical issue that may preclude your enlistment. During this meeting, the recruiter will discuss which branch(es) of service you qualify for and possible career options for you to choose from.

After selecting an MOS, you and your recruiter can discuss entry dates for your basic training and enroll you in online training courses to introduce you to the military and prepare you for basic training. While going through the testing and online training, your recruiter is your main contact until the date you take the oath of enlistment. Your recruiter can answer any concerns or questions you have along the way.

PRACTICE TEST ONE

GENERAL SCIENCE

This part of the test measures your knowledge in the area of science. Each of the questions or incomplete statements is followed by four choices. You are to decide which one of the choices best answers the question or completes the statement.

1. Bone is composed primarily of which inorganic material?
    (A) calcium
    (B) phosphorus
    (C) collagen
    (D) potassium

2. Which of these is a biome?
    (A) a desert
    (B) a cornfield
    (C) a herd of bison
    (D) a beehive

3. Which planet orbits closest to Earth?
    (A) Mercury
    (B) Venus
    (C) Jupiter
    (D) Saturn

4. What is the name of the phenomenon when a star suddenly increases in brightness and then disappears from view?
    (A) aurora
    (B) galaxy
    (C) black hole
    (D) supernova

5. Which organism has cells that contain mitochondria?
    (A) whale
    (B) mushroom
    (C) tulip
    (D) all of the above

6. Isotopes of an element will have the same number of _____ and different numbers of _____.
    (A) electrons; neutrons
    (B) neutrons; electrons
    (C) protons; neutrons
    (D) protons; electrons

7. Which condition can be diagnosed by an electrocardiogram (EKG)?
   (A) diabetes
   (B) torn ligaments
   (C) cancer
   (D) tachycardia

8. What are the negatively charged particles inside an atom?
   (A) protons
   (B) neutrons
   (C) electrons
   (D) ions

9. Which organism regulates its body temperature externally?
   (A) lobster
   (B) dolphin
   (C) whale
   (D) pelican

10. A box sliding down a ramp experiences all of the following forces EXCEPT
    (A) tension.
    (B) friction.
    (C) gravity.
    (D) normal.

11. Which organism is a decomposer?
    (A) apple trees
    (B) mushrooms
    (C) goats
    (D) lions

12. Which pH level is classified as a base?
    (A) 1
    (B) 4
    (C) 6
    (D) 8

13. Which body system is responsible for the release of growth hormones?
    (A) digestive system
    (B) endocrine system
    (C) nervous system
    (D) circulatory system

14. What is the term for the top layer of the earth's surface?
    (A) exosphere
    (B) lithosphere
    (C) atmosphere
    (D) biosphere

15. Which of the following describes a physical change?
    (A) Water becomes ice.
    (B) Batter is baked into a cake.
    (C) An iron fence rusts.
    (D) A firecracker explodes.

16. Which energy source is nonrenewable?
    (A) water
    (B) wind
    (C) coal
    (D) sunlight

17. How long does it take the earth to rotate on its axis?
    (A) one hour
    (B) one day
    (C) one month
    (D) one year

18. During what process do producers make sugars and release oxygen?
    (A) digestion
    (B) chloroplast
    (C) decomposition
    (D) photosynthesis

19. $2C_6H_{14} + 19O_2 \rightarrow 12CO_2 + 14H_2O$

What type of reaction is shown above?

(A) substitution reaction
(B) acid-base reaction
(C) decomposition reaction
(D) combustion reaction

20. Which factor is an abiotic part of an ecosystem?

(A) producers
(B) consumers
(C) water
(D) decomposers

21. What is the primary function of the respiratory system?

(A) to create sound and speech
(B) to take oxygen into the body while removing carbon dioxide
(C) to transport nutrients to the cells and tissue of the body
(D) to act as a barrier between the body's organs and foreign pathogens

22. The process of organisms with advantageous traits surviving more often and producing more offspring than organisms without these advantageous traits describes which basic mechanism of evolution?

(A) gene flow
(B) genetic drift
(C) mutation
(D) natural selection

23. Which muscular organ processes food material into smaller pieces and helps mix it with saliva?

(A) pharynx
(B) tongue
(C) diaphragm
(D) stomach

24. Which of the following correctly describes a strong acid?

(A) A strong acid completely ionizes in water.
(B) A strong acid donates more than one proton.
(C) A strong acid has a pH close to 7.
(D) A strong acid will not ionize.

25. Which action is an example of mechanical weathering?

(A) Calcium carbonate reacts with water to form a cave.
(B) An iron gate rusts.
(C) Tree roots grow under the foundation of a house and cause cracks.
(D) Bananas turn brown after they are peeled.

ARITHMETIC REASONING

This part of the test measures your ability to use arithmetic to solve problems. Each problem is followed by four possible answers. You are to decide which one of the four choices is correct.

1. A high school cross country team sent 25 percent of its runners to a regional competition. Of these, 10 percent won medals. If 2 runners earned medals, how many members does the cross country team have?
   - (A) 8
   - (B) 10
   - (C) 80
   - (D) 125

2. Convert 55 meters to feet (round to the nearest tenth of a foot).
   - (A) 16.8 feet
   - (B) 21.7 feet
   - (C) 139.7 feet
   - (D) 180.4 feet

3. If a person reads 40 pages in 45 minutes, approximately how many minutes will it take her to read 265 pages?
   - (A) 202
   - (B) 236
   - (C) 265
   - (D) 298

4. If three burgers and two orders of fries costs $26.50 and a burger costs $6.50, how much does one order of fries cost?
   - (A) $1.75
   - (B) $3.50
   - (C) $6.75
   - (D) $7.00

5. A worker was paid $15,036 for 7 months of work. If he received the same amount each month, how much was he paid for the first 2 months?
   - (A) $2,148
   - (B) $4,296
   - (C) $5,137
   - (D) $6,444

6. The average speed of cars on a highway (s) is inversely proportional to the number of cars on the road (n). If a car drives at 65 mph when there are 250 cars on the road, how fast will a car drive when there are 325 cars on the road?
   - (A) 50 mph
   - (B) 55 mph
   - (C) 60 mph
   - (D) 85 mph

7. The probability of drawing a blue marble from a bag of marbles is $\frac{1}{20}$ and the probability of drawing a red marble from the same bag is $\frac{7}{20}$. What is the probability of drawing a blue marble or a red marble?
   - (A) $\frac{1}{10}$
   - (B) $\frac{3}{10}$
   - (C) $\frac{7}{20}$
   - (D) $\frac{2}{5}$

8. The population of a town was 7,250 in 2014 and 7,375 in 2015. What was the percent increase from 2014 to 2015 to the nearest tenth of a percent?

(A) 1.5%
(B) 1.6%
(C) 1.7%
(D) 1.8%

9. Lynn has 4 test scores in science class. Each test is worth 100 points, and Lynn has an 85% average. If Lynn scored 100% on each of the first 3 tests, what did she score on her 4th test?

(A) 40%
(B) 55%
(C) 60%
(D) 85%

10. Allison used $2\frac{1}{2}$ cups of flour to make a cake, and $\frac{3}{4}$ of a cup of flour to make a pie. If she started with 4 cups of flour, how many cups of flour does she have left?

(A) $\frac{3}{4}$
(B) 1
(C) $\frac{5}{4}$
(D) $\frac{5}{2}$

11. Alex cleans houses and charges $25 per bedroom, $35 per bathroom, and $40 per kitchen. If he cleans a house with 4 bedrooms, 2 bathrooms, and 1 kitchen, how much will he be paid?

(A) $205
(B) $210
(C) $215
(D) $230

12. Juan plans to spend 25% of his workday writing a report. If he is at work for 9 hours, how many hours will he spend writing the report?

(A) 2.25
(B) 2.50
(C) 2.75
(D) 3.25

13. Valerie receives a base salary of $740 a week for working 40 hours. For every extra hour she works, she is paid at a rate of $27.75 per hour. If Valerie works t hours in a week, which of the following equations represents the amount of money, A, she will receive?

(A) $A = 740 + 27.75(t - 40)$
(B) $A = 740 + 27.75(40 - t)$
(C) $A = 740 - 27.75(40 - t)$
(D) $A = 27.75t - 740$

14. If $\triangle ABD \sim \triangle DEF$ and the similarity ratio is 3:4, what is the measure of DE if $AB = 12$?

(A) 6
(B) 9
(C) 12
(D) 16

15. Justin has a summer lawn care business and earns $40 for each lawn he mows. He also pays $35 per week in business expenses. Which of the following expressions represents Justin's profit after x weeks if he mows m number of lawns?

(A) $40m - 35x$
(B) $40m + 35x$
(C) $35x(40 + m)$
(D) $35(40m + x)$

16. Micah has invited 23 friends to his house and is having pizza for dinner. If each pizza feeds 4 people, how many pizzas should he order?

(A) 4
(B) 5
(C) 6
(D) 7

17. In the fall, 425 students pass the math benchmark. In the spring, 680 students pass the same benchmark. What is the percentage increase in passing scores from fall to spring?

(A) 37.5%
(B) 55%
(C) 60%
(D) 62.5%

18. Maria paid $24.65 for her meal at a restaurant. If that price included a tax of 8.25 percent, what was the price of the meal before tax?

(A) $22.61
(B) $22.68
(C) $22.77
(D) $22.82

19. A high school football team played 12 games in a season. If they won 75 percent of their games, how many games did they lose?

(A) 3
(B) 4
(C) 6
(D) 9

20. A fruit stand sells apples, bananas, and oranges at a ratio of 3:2:1. If the fruit stand sells 20 bananas, how many total pieces of fruit does the fruit stand sell?

(A) 10
(B) 30
(C) 40
(D) 60

21. Aprille has $50 to buy the items on her shopping list. Assuming there is no sales tax, about how much change will Aprille receive after buying all the items on her list?

Aprille's List

ITEM	PRICE
Hammer	$13.24
Screwdriver	$11.99
Nails	$4.27
Wrench	$5.60

(A) $12
(B) $13
(C) $14
(D) $15

22. A company interviewed 21 applicants for a recent opening. Of these applicants, 7 wore blue and 6 wore white, while 5 applicants wore both blue and white. What is the number of applicants who wore neither blue nor white?

(A) 1
(B) 6
(C) 8
(D) 13

23. In the sequence below, each term is found by finding the difference between the previous two numbers and multiplying the result by −3. What is the 6th term of the sequence?

{3, 0, −9, −36, ...}

(A) −81
(B) −135
(C) 45
(D) 81

24. If the length of a rectangle is increased by 40% and its width is decreased by 40%, what is the effect on the rectangle's area?

(A) The area is the same.
(B) It increases by 16%.
(C) It increases by 20%.
(D) It decreases by 16%.

25. If a plane travels 2,775 miles in 3 hours, how far will it travel in 5 hours?

(A) 1,665 miles
(B) 3,475 miles
(C) 4,625 miles
(D) 5,550 miles

26. A theater has 180 rows of seats. The first row has 10 seats. Each row has 4 seats more than the row in front of it. How many seats are in the entire theater?

(A) 18,000
(B) 20,000
(C) 36,200
(D) 66,240

27. Erica is at work for $8\frac{1}{2}$ hours a day. If she takes one 30-minute lunch break and two 15-minute breaks during the day, how many hours does she work?

(A) 6 hours, 30 minutes
(B) 6 hours, 45 minutes
(C) 7 hours, 15 minutes
(D) 7 hours, 30 minutes

28. At the grocery store, apples cost $1.89 per pound and oranges cost $2.19 per pound. How much would it cost to purchase 2 pounds of apples and 1.5 pounds of oranges?

(A) $6.62
(B) $7.07
(C) $7.14
(D) $7.22

29. A car traveled at 65 miles per hour for $1\frac{1}{2}$ hours and then traveled at 50 miles per hour for $2\frac{1}{2}$ hours. How many miles did the car travel?

(A) 190.5 miles
(B) 215.0 miles
(C) 222.5 miles
(D) 237.5 miles

30. What is the square root of 169?

(A) 9
(B) 13
(C) 16
(D) 19

WORD KNOWLEDGE

This part of the test measures your knowledge of words and their meanings. For each question, you are to choose the word below that is closest in meaning to the capitalized word above.

1. Pacify most nearly means
   - (A) soothe.
   - (B) transport.
   - (C) bathe.
   - (D) motivate.

2. The judge ruled that certain facts were immaterial to the case, so she would not allow the prosecutor to use those facts as evidence.
   - (A) invisible
   - (B) opposed
   - (C) offensive
   - (D) inconsequential

3. The man flagrantly broke several laws, so he was easily convicted and sent to prison.
   - (A) joyously
   - (B) unashamedly
   - (C) incautiously
   - (D) mistakenly

4. Indolence most nearly means
   - (A) serenity.
   - (B) bliss.
   - (C) laziness.
   - (D) tolerance.

5. When a strange dog ran into the room, the cat made the judicious decision to jump onto the top of the bookcase.
   - (A) wise.
   - (B) quick.
   - (C) weird.
   - (D) brave.

6. Pragmatic most nearly means
   - (A) accurate.
   - (B) tedious.
   - (C) realistic.
   - (D) imaginative.

7. Countenance most nearly means
   - (A) total amount.
   - (B) fancy clothing.
   - (C) body language.
   - (D) facial expression.

8. Cacophony most nearly means
   - (A) harsh sound.
   - (B) melodious music.
   - (C) synthetic product.
   - (D) artificial flavor.

9. Charisma most nearly means
   - (A) love.
   - (B) motion.
   - (C) sneakiness.
   - (D) attractiveness.

10. My aunt has a capricious nature, so we never know whether she will or will not show up at family celebrations.
    - (A) voluminous
    - (B) materialistic
    - (C) unreliable
    - (D) intolerable

11. Daunt most nearly means
    - (A) thrill.
    - (B) shove.
    - (C) intimidate.
    - (D) encourage.

12. The theater's new production received great <u>acclaim</u> from newspaper critics.
    (A) pity.
    (B) praise.
    (C) notoriety.
    (D) interest.

13. <u>Credulous</u> most nearly means
    (A) naïve.
    (B) amazing.
    (C) tedious.
    (D) optimistic.

14. Rotary telephones are <u>obsolete</u>, and almost no one uses them anymore.
    (A) unsafe
    (B) old-fashioned
    (C) too bulky
    (D) too heavy

15. <u>Labyrinth</u> most nearly means
    (A) maze.
    (B) dungeon.
    (C) workshop.
    (D) basement.

16. <u>Sacrosanct</u> most nearly means
    (A) handy.
    (B) quiet.
    (C) secure.
    (D) holy.

17. My sister has an <u>effervescent</u> personality, so everyone invites her to their parties to liven them up.
    (A) jumpy
    (B) vivacious
    (C) eternal
    (D) suspicious

18. <u>Rudimentary</u> most nearly means
    (A) impolite.
    (B) basic.
    (C) juvenile.
    (D) innovative.

19. Showing deep emotion, the conductor flourished his baton, directing the orchestra with <u>fervor</u>.
    (A) indifference
    (B) swiftness
    (C) grace
    (D) eagerness

20. To <u>cajole</u> most nearly means to
    (A) persuade.
    (B) cheer up.
    (C) imprison.
    (D) compel.

21. <u>Impartial</u> most nearly means
    (A) fond.
    (B) incomplete.
    (C) objective.
    (D) mathematical.

22. A mountain peak may seem <u>immutable</u>, but erosion may wear it down over thousands of years.
    (A) gigantic
    (B) awesome
    (C) unalterable
    (D) insensible

23. <u>Reiterate</u> most nearly means
    (A) recite.
    (B) repeat.
    (C) reunite.
    (D) reread.

PRACTICE TEST ONE

24. The politician gave a long, bombastic speech that was full of pretentious language.
    (A) folksy
    (B) exploding
    (C) pompous
    (D) eloquent

25. Precedent most nearly means
    (A) event.
    (B) birth.
    (C) idea.
    (D) model.

26. Prudent most nearly means
    (A) sensible.
    (B) inquisitive.
    (C) terrified.
    (D) squeamish.

27. The office is organized in a haphazard manner, so it is next to impossible to find anything quickly.
    (A) dangerous
    (B) precise
    (C) chaotic
    (D) cautious

28. Figurative most nearly means
    (A) lofty.
    (B) lengthy.
    (C) nonliteral.
    (D) uncooperative.

29. Innocuous most nearly means
    (A) susceptible.
    (B) sickly.
    (C) bland.
    (D) cautious.

30. Shelby *is* the club president, but I sometimes wish she were not so officious—I get tired of her bossy manner.
    (A) resourceful
    (B) emotional
    (C) detail-oriented
    (D) overbearing

31. Negligence most nearly means
    (A) malice.
    (B) immorality.
    (C) inattention.
    (D) nothingness.

32. Lax most nearly means
    (A) decorative.
    (B) malicious.
    (C) meddlesome.
    (D) permissive.

33. My dog is always meandering around the yard, smelling every scent she can detect.
    (A) digging
    (B) relaxing
    (C) sprinting
    (D) wandering

34. Ardent most nearly means
    (A) silvery.
    (B) stubborn.
    (C) metallic.
    (D) passionate.

35. Whenever she wears a certain jacket, my sister garners compliments from everyone she meets.
    (A) awards
    (B) enjoys
    (C) collects
    (D) improves

Paragraph Comprehension

This part of the test measures your ability to read and understand written material. Each passage is followed by a multiple-choice question. You are to choose the option that best answers the question based on the passage. No additional information or specific knowledge is needed.

In December of 1945, Germany launched its last major offensive campaign of World War II, pushing through the dense forests of the Ardennes region of Belgium, France, and Luxembourg. The attack, designed to block the Allies from the Belgian port of Antwerp and to split their lines, caught the Allied forces by surprise. Due to troop positioning, the Americans bore the brunt of the attack, incurring 100,000 deaths, the highest number of casualties of any battle during the war. However, after a month of grueling fighting in the bitter cold, a lack of fuel and a masterful American military strategy resulted in an Allied victory that sealed Germany's fate.

1. In the last sentence, the word *grueling* most nearly means
   - (A) exhausting.
   - (B) costly.
   - (C) intermittent.
   - (D) ineffective.

The social and political discourse of America continues to be permeated with idealism. An idealistic viewpoint asserts that the ideals of freedom, equality, justice, and human dignity are the truths that Americans must continue to aspire to. Idealists argue that truth is what should be, not necessarily what is. In general, they work to improve things and to make them as close to ideal as possible.

2. The primary purpose of the passage is to
   - (A) advocate for freedom, equality, justice, and human rights.
   - (B) explain what an idealist believes in.
   - (C) explain what's wrong with social and political discourse in America.
   - (D) persuade readers to believe in certain truths.

The greatest changes in sensory, motor, and perceptual development happen in the first two years of life. When babies are first born, most of their senses operate in a similar way to those of adults. For example, babies are able to hear before they are born; studies show that babies turn toward the sound of their mothers' voices just minutes after being born, indicating they recognize the mother's voice from their time in the womb.

The exception to this rule is vision. A baby's vision changes significantly in its first year of life; initially it has a range of vision of only 8–12 inches and no depth perception. As a result, infants rely primarily on hearing; vision does not become the dominant sense until around the age of 12 months. Babies also prefer faces to other objects. This preference, along with their limited vision range, means that their sight is initially focused on their caregiver.

3. Which of the following senses do babies primarily rely on?
   - (A) vision
   - (B) hearing
   - (C) touch
   - (D) smell

Tourists flock to Yellowstone National Park each year to view the geysers that bubble and erupt throughout it. What most of these tourists do not know is that these geysers are formed by a caldera, a hot crater in the earth's crust, that was created by a series of three eruptions of an ancient supervolcano. These eruptions, which began 2.1 million years ago, spewed between 1,000 to 2,450 cubic kilometers of volcanic matter at such a rate that the volcano's magma chamber collapsed, creating the craters.

4. The main idea of the passage is that
    (A) Yellowstone National Park is a popular tourist destination.
    (B) The geysers in Yellowstone National Park rest on a caldera in the earth's crust.
    (C) A supervolcano once sat in the area covered by Yellowstone National Park.
    (D) The earth's crust is weaker in Yellowstone National Park.

In 1989, almost a million Chinese university students descended on central Beijing, protesting for increased democracy and calling for the resignation of Communist Party leaders. For three weeks, they marched, chanted, and held daily vigils in the city's Tiananmen Square. The protests had widespread support in China, particularly among factory workers who cheered them on. For Westerners watching, it seemed to be the beginning of a political revolution in China, so the world was stunned when, on July 4, Chinese troops and security police stormed the square, firing into the crowd. Chaos erupted with some students trying to fight back by throwing stones and setting fire to military vehicles. Tens of thousands more attempted to flee. While official numbers were never given, observers estimated anywhere from 300 to thousands of people were killed, while 10,000 were arrested.

5. It can be inferred from the passage that after July 4
    (A) the protest movement in China gained increasing support.
    (B) Western countries intervened on behalf of the university protestors.
    (C) factory workers took action in defense of the protestors.
    (D) the movement for increased democracy in China fell apart.

The Battle of Little Bighorn, commonly called Custer's Last Stand, was a battle between the Lakota, the Northern Cheyenne, the Arapaho, and the Seventh Calvary Regiment of the US Army. Led by war leaders Crazy Horse and Chief Gall and the religious leader Sitting Bull, the allied tribes of the Plains Indians decisively defeated their US foes. Two hundred and sixty-eight US soldiers were killed, including General George Armstrong Custer, two of his brothers, his nephew, his brother-in-law, and six Indian scouts.

6. What is the main idea of this passage?
    (A) Most of General Custer's family died in the Battle of Little Bighorn.
    (B) The Seventh Calvary regiment was formed to fight Native American tribes.
    (C) Sitting Bull and George Custer were fierce enemies.
    (D) The Battle of Little Bighorn was a significant victory for the Plains Indians.

At first glance, the landscape of the northern end of the Rift Valley appears to be a stretch of barren land. Paleoanthropologists, however, have discovered an abundance of fossils just beneath the dusty surface. They believe this area once contained open grasslands near lakes and rivers, populated with grazing animals. Forty miles from this spot, in 1974, scientists uncovered a 3.2 million-year-old non-human hominid they nicknamed "Lucy." And, in 2013, researchers found the oldest fossil in the human ancestral line. Before this, the oldest fossil from the genus

Homo—of which *Homo sapiens* are the only remaining species—dated only back to 2.3 million years ago, leaving a 700,000 gap between Lucy's species and the advent of humans. The new fossil dated back to 2.75 and 2.8 million years ago, pushing the appearance of humans back 400,000 years.

7. According to the passage, the discovery of Lucy
    (A) gave scientists new information about the development of humans.
    (B) provided evidence of a different ecosystem in the ancient Rift Valley.
    (C) supported the belief that other hominids existed significantly before humans.
    (D) closed the gap between the development of other hominids and humans.

In its most basic form, geography is the study of space; more specifically, it studies the physical space of the earth and the ways in which it interacts with, shapes, and is shaped by its habitants. Geographers look at the world from a spatial perspective. This means that at the center of all geographic study is the question, *where?* For geographers, the *where* of any interaction, event, or development is a crucial element to understanding it.

This question of *where* can be asked in a variety of fields of study, so there are many sub-disciplines of geography. These can be organized into four main categories: 1) regional studies, which examine the characteristics of a particular place; 2) topical studies, which look at a single physical or human feature that impacts the whole world; 3) physical studies, which focus on the physical features of Earth; and 4) human studies, which examine the relationship between human activity and the environment.

8. A researcher studying the relationship between farming and river systems would be engaged in which of the following geographical sub-disciplines?
    (A) regional studies
    (B) topical studies
    (C) physical studies
    (D) human studies

Researchers at the University of California, Berkeley, decided to tackle an age-old problem: why shoelaces come untied. They recorded the shoelaces of a volunteer walking on a treadmill by attaching devices to record the acceleration, or g-force, experienced by the knot. The results were surprising. A shoelace knot experiences more g-force from a person walking than any rollercoaster can generate. However, if the person simply stomped or swung their feet—the two movements that make up a walker's stride—the g-force was not enough to undo the knots. Researchers also found that while the knot loosened slowly at first, once it reached a certain laxness, it simply fell apart.

9. The author includes a comparison to rollercoasters in order to
    (A) illustrate the intensity of force experienced by the knots.
    (B) describe an experiment undertaken by researchers.
    (C) critique a main finding of the experiment.
    (D) provide further evidence to support the study's conclusion.

In 1953, doctors surgically removed the hippocampus of patient Henry Molaison in an attempt to stop his frequent seizures. Unexpectedly, he lost the ability to form new memories, leading to the biggest breakthrough in the science of memory. Molaison's long-term memory—of events more than a year before his surgery—was unchanged as was his ability to learn physical skills. From this, scientists learned that different types of memory are handled by different parts of the brain, with the hippocampus responsible for *episodic memory*, the short-term recall of events. They have since discovered that some memories are then channeled to the cortex, the outer layers of the brain that handle higher functions, where they are gradually integrated with related information to build lasting knowledge about our world.

10. The main idea of the passage is that

(A) Molaison's surgery posed significant risk to the functioning of his brain.

(B) short-term and long-term memory are stored in different parts of the brain.

(C) long-term memory forms over a longer period than short-term memory.

(D) memories of physical skills are processed differently than memories of events.

After World War I, powerful political and social forces pushed for a return to normalcy in the United States. The result was disengagement from the larger world and increased focus on American economic growth and personal enjoyment. Caught in the middle of this was a cache of American writers, raised on the values of the prewar world and frustrated with what they viewed as the superficiality and materialism of postwar American culture. Many of them, like Ernest Hemingway and F. Scott Fitzgerald, fled to Paris, where they became known as the "lost generation," creating a trove of literary works criticizing their home culture and delving into their own feelings of alienation.

11. In the third sentence, the word *cache* most nearly means

(A) a group of the same type.

(B) a majority segment.

(C) an organization.

(D) a dispersed number.

When the Spanish-American War broke out in 1898, the US Army was small and understaffed. President William McKinley called for 1,250 volunteers primarily from the Southwest to serve in the First US Volunteer Calvary. Eager to fight, the ranks were quickly filled by a diverse group of cowboys, gold prospectors, hunters, gamblers, Native Americans, veterans, police officers, and college students looking for an adventure. The officer corps was composed of veterans of the Civil War and the Indian Wars. With more volunteers than it could accept, the army set high standards: all the recruits had to be skilled on horseback and with guns. Consequently, they became known as the Rough Riders.

12. According to the passage, all the recruits were required to

(A) have previously fought in a war.

(B) be American citizens.

(C) live in the Southwest.

(D) ride a horse well.

It could be said that the great battle between the North and South we call the Civil War was a battle for individual identity. The states of the South had their own culture, one based on farming, independence, and the rights of both man and state to determine their own paths. Similarly, the North had forged its own identity as a center of centralized commerce and manufacturing. This clash of lifestyles was bound to create tension, and this tension was bound to lead to war. But people who try to sell you this narrative are wrong. The Civil War was not a battle of cultural identities—it was a battle about slavery. All other explanations for the war are either a direct consequence of the South's desire for wealth at the expense of her fellow man or a fanciful invention to cover up this sad portion of our nation's history. And it cannot be denied that this time in our past was very sad indeed.

13. What is the main idea of the passage?
    (A) The Civil War was the result of cultural differences between the North and South.
    (B) The Civil War was caused by the South's reliance on slave labor.
    (C) The North's use of commerce and manufacturing allowed it to win the war.
    (D) The South's belief in the rights of man and state cost the war.

When a fire destroyed San Francisco's American Indian Center in October of 1969, American Indian groups set their sights on the recently closed island prison of Alcatraz as a site of a new Indian cultural center and school. Ignored by the government, an activist group known as Indians of All Tribes sailed to Alcatraz in the early morning hours with eighty-nine men, women, and children. They landed on Alcatraz, claiming it for all the tribes of North America. Their demands were ignored, and so the group continued to occupy the island for the next nineteen months, its numbers swelling up to 600 as others joined. By January of 1970, many of the original protestors had left, and on June 11, 1971, federal marshals forcibly removed the last residents.

14. The main idea of this passage is that
    (A) the government refused to listen to the demands of American Indians.
    (B) American Indians occupied Alcatraz in protest of government policy.
    (C) few people joined the occupation of Alcatraz, weakening its effectiveness.
    (D) the government took violent action against protestors at Alcatraz.

The Bastille, Paris's famous historical prison, was originally built in 1370 as a fortification, called a *bastide* in Old French, to protect the city from English invasion during the Hundred Years' War. It rose 100 feet into the air, had eight towers, and was surrounded by a moat more than eighty feet wide. In the seventeenth century, the government converted the fortress into an elite prison for upper-class felons, political disruptors, and spies. Residents of the Bastille arrived by direct order of the king and usually were left there to languish without a trial.

15. In the first sentence, the word *fortification* most nearly means
    (A) royal castle.
    (B) national symbol.
    (C) seat of government.
    (D) defensive structure.

MATH KNOWLEDGE

This part of the test measures your knowledge of mathematical terms and principles. Each problem is followed by four possible answers. You are to decide which one of the four choices is correct.

1. Which of the following is equivalent to $z^3(z + 2)^2 - 4z^3 + 2$?
   (A) 2
   (B) $z^5 + 4z^4 + 4z^3 + 2$
   (C) $z^6 + 4z^3 + 2$
   (D) $z^5 + 4z^4 + 2$

2. Simplify: $\dfrac{(3x^2y^2)^2}{3^3x^{-2}y^3}$
   (A) $3x^6y$
   (B) $\dfrac{x^6y}{3}$
   (C) $\dfrac{x^4}{3y}$
   (D) $\dfrac{3x^4}{y}$

3. What is the value of $\left(\dfrac{1}{2}\right)^3$?
   (A) $\dfrac{1}{8}$
   (B) $\dfrac{1}{6}$
   (C) $\dfrac{1}{4}$
   (D) $\dfrac{3}{8}$

4. How many cubic feet of soil would be required to cover a circular garden with a diameter of 8 feet if the soil needs to be 0.5 feet deep (use $\pi = 3.14$)?
   (A) 6.28 ft³
   (B) 12.56 ft³
   (C) 25.12 ft³
   (D) 100.48 ft³

5. Which of the following sets of shapes are NOT all similar to each other?
   (A) right triangles
   (B) spheres
   (C) 30–60–90 triangles
   (D) squares

6. The line of best fit is calculated for a data set that tracks the number of miles that passenger cars traveled annually in the US from 1960 to 2010. In the model, $x = 0$ represents the year 1960, and y is the number of miles traveled in billions. If the line of best fit is $y = 0.0293x + 0.563$, approximately how many additional miles were traveled for every 5 years that passed?
   (A) 0.0293 billion
   (B) 0.1465 billion
   (C) 0.5630 billion
   (D) 0.7100 billion
   (E) 2.9615 billion

7. Simplify: $\sqrt[3]{64} + \sqrt[3]{729}$
   (A) 13
   (B) 15
   (C) 17
   (D) 31

8. What is the remainder when 397 is divided by 4?
   (A) 0
   (B) 1
   (C) 2
   (D) 3

9. If the surface area of a cylinder with radius of 4 feet is 48π square feet, what is its volume?
   (A) 1π ft.³
   (B) 16π ft.³
   (C) 32π ft.³
   (D) 48π ft.³

10. Which expression is equivalent to $(x + 3)(x - 2)(x + 4)$?
  - (A) $x^3 - 2x + 24$
  - (B) $x^3 + 5x - 24$
  - (C) $x^3 + 9x^2 - 24$
  - (D) $x^3 + 5x^2 - 2x - 24$

11. Which of the following is a solution of the given equation?
$4(m + 4)^2 - 4m^2 + 20 = 276$
  - (A) 3
  - (B) 4
  - (C) 6
  - (D) 12

12. What is the x-intercept of the given equation?
$10x + 10y = 10$
  - (A) (1, 0)
  - (B) (0, 1)
  - (C) (0, 0)
  - (D) (1, 1)

13. Which of the following is closest in value to $129{,}113 + 34{,}602$?
  - (A) 162,000
  - (B) 163,000
  - (C) 164,000
  - (D) 165,000

14. Solve for x: $x^2 - 3x - 18 = 0$
  - (A) $x = -3$
  - (B) $x = 2$
  - (C) $x = -3$ and $x = 6$
  - (D) $x = 2$ and $x = 3$

15. The coordinates of point A are $(7, 12)$ and the coordinates of point C are $(-3, 10)$. If C is the midpoint of $\overline{AB}$, what are the coordinates of point B?
  - (A) $(-13, 8)$
  - (B) $(-13, 11)$
  - (C) $(2, 11)$
  - (D) $(2, 14)$

16. Which of the following could be the perimeter of a triangle with two sides that measure 13 and 5?
  - (A) 24.5
  - (B) 26.5
  - (C) 36
  - (D) 37

17. What is $\frac{5}{8}$ as a percent?
  - (A) 1.6%
  - (B) 16%
  - (C) 0.625%
  - (D) 62.5%

18. What is the value of z in the following system?
$z - 2x = 14$
$2z - 6x = 18$
  - (A) -7
  - (B) -2
  - (C) 3
  - (D) 24

19. What is the value of the expression $15m + 2n^2 - 7$ if $m = 3$ and $n = -4$?
  - (A) -49
  - (B) -31
  - (C) 6
  - (D) 70

20. Which number has the greatest value?
  - (A) 9,299 ones
  - (B) 903 tens
  - (C) 93 hundreds
  - (D) 9 thousands

21. Which of the following is an equation of the line that passes through the points (4, −3) and (−2, 9) in the *xy*-plane?

    (A) $y = -2x + 5$
    (B) $y = -\frac{1}{2}x - 1$
    (C) $y = \frac{1}{2}x - 5$
    (D) $y = 2x - 11$

22. *W*, *X*, *Y*, and *Z* lie on a circle with center *A*. If the diameter of the circle is 75, what is the sum of $\overline{AW}$, $\overline{AX}$, $\overline{AY}$, and $\overline{AZ}$?

    (A) 75
    (B) 100
    (C) 125
    (D) 150

23. Which inequality is equivalent to $10 \leq k - 5$?

    (A) $k \leq 15$
    (B) $k \geq 15$
    (C) $k \leq 5$
    (D) $k \geq 5$

24. Rectangular water tank A is 5 feet long, 10 feet wide, and 4 feet tall. Rectangular tank B is 5 feet long, 5 feet wide, and 4 feet tall. If the same amount of water is poured into both tanks and the height of the water in Tank A is 1 foot, how high will the water be in Tank B?

    (A) 1 foot
    (B) 2 feet
    (C) 3 feet
    (D) 4 feet

25. The inequality $2a - 5b > 12$ is true for which values of *a* and *b*?

    (A) $a = 2$ and $b = 6$
    (B) $a = 1$ and $b = -3$
    (C) $a = -1$ and $b = 3$
    (D) $a = 7$ and $b = 2$

Electronics

This part of the test measures your knowledge of electronics. Each of the questions or incomplete statements is followed by four choices. You are to decide which one of the choices best answers the question or completes the statement.

1. An atom has 5 electrons and 12 protons. What is the total charge of the atom?
   (A) −17e
   (B) −7e
   (C) +7e
   (D) +17e

2. Power is measured in
   (A) watts.
   (B) amperes.
   (C) joules.
   (D) ohms.

3. Valence electrons are important in a circuit because they
   (A) can easily change between positive and negative charge.
   (B) allow protons to flow through the circuit, creating current.
   (C) are stored in the circuit's voltage source.
   (D) carry the charge in conducting materials.

4. Conventional current is
   (A) a naming convention that states that current is in the same direction as the movement of electrons.
   (B) a naming convention that states that current is in the same direction as the movement of positive charge, or holes.
   (C) another name for direct current.
   (D) another name for alternating current.

5. A circuit with one 5 Ω resistor has a current of 0.5 A. How much voltage is being applied to the circuit?
   (A) 0.1 V
   (B) 2.5 V
   (C) 10 V
   (D) 25 V

6. What is the source of the electromotive force, EMF, in a battery?
   (A) The is no EMF from a battery.
   (B) mechanical movement
   (C) changing magnetic field
   (D) chemical reactions

7. If the current flowing through a fuse is too high, how does a fuse protect a circuit?
   (A) The metal element in the fuse will overheat and vaporize, breaking the circuit.
   (B) The metal element in the fuse will overheat and oxidize, leading to a higher and higher resistance in the fuse.
   (C) The fuse has a built-in switch that will flip to break the circuit. The switch needs to be manually flipped back to reconnect the circuit.
   (D) The fuse will automatically lower the current value to an acceptable level if it gets too high.

8. The symbol below is used to represent which part of a circuit?

   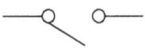

   (A) diode
   (B) switch
   (C) fuse
   (D) battery

9. If a voltmeter measures 10 V across a resistor and an ammeter measures 5 mA going through it, what would an ohmmeter measure as the resistance of the resistor?

   (A) 500 Ω
   (B) 1 kΩ
   (C) 1.5 kΩ
   (D) 2 kΩ

10. Find the equivalent resistance, R_{eq}, for the circuit in the figure below.

    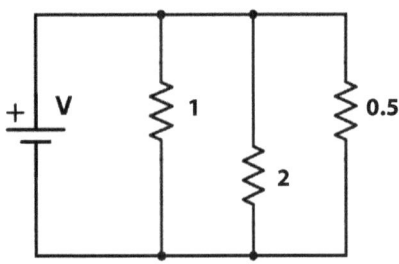

    (A) 0.3 kΩ
    (B) 0.5 kΩ
    (C) 2 kΩ
    (D) 3.5 kΩ

11. What application would use a variable resistor?

    (A) a dimmer for a light bulb
    (B) a regular switch for a light bulb
    (C) a doorbell button
    (D) a key on a computer keyboard

12. What is the basic function of a capacitor?

    (A) It acts as a switch.
    (B) It stores energy.
    (C) It only allows current in one direction.
    (D) It is the heating element in an oven.

13. What is the most common use of a transistor?

    (A) a solid-state switch
    (B) a solid-state capacitor
    (C) a solid-state solenoid
    (D) a solid-state laser

14. Which application would be a proper use of a rectifier circuit?

    (A) transforming a 100 V signal into a 200 V signal
    (B) transforming a 200 V signal into a 100 V signal
    (C) converting the AC output from an alternator into a DC signal
    (D) converting the DC output from a dynamo into an AC signal

15. How does an inductor behave in a circuit?

    (A) It acts as an antenna.
    (B) It produces sound.
    (C) It resists a change in current.
    (D) It converts AC into DC.

16. A customer needs a motor that rotates in a full circle 60 times per second (60 Hz). The motor will be connected to an AC power supply that has a frequency of 60 Hz. What type of motor is it?

    (A) synchronous motor
    (B) asynchronous motor
    (C) high-speed motor
    (D) low-torque motor

17. What is the stator field?
- **(A)** the magnetic field created by permanent magnets or electromagnets in the stator
- **(B)** the electric field created by permanent charges or electromagnets in the stator
- **(C)** the magnetic field created by permanent magnets in the rotor
- **(D)** the electric field created by permanent charges in the rotor

18. Electrical power suppliers produce power at high voltage to transfer power over long distances, and the voltage is reduced to the value (120 V) used in homes and offices. What device is used to make this reduction?
- **(A)** alternator
- **(B)** transformer
- **(C)** rectifier
- **(D)** capacitor

19. What is the current flowing through a 15 Ω resistor when 120 V is applied to the circuit?
- **(A)** 80 mA
- **(B)** 125 mA
- **(C)** 8 A
- **(D)** 12.5 A

20. All of the following store energy EXCEPT
- **(A)** capacitor.
- **(B)** battery.
- **(C)** inductor.
- **(D)** transformer.

Automotive and Shop Information

This part of the test measures your knowledge of automotive and shop information. Each of the questions or incomplete statements is followed by four choices. You are to decide which one of the choices best answers the question or completes the statement.

1. When does combustion happen?
   - (A) when air enters the cylinder
   - (B) when the air and fuel mixture has cooled down
   - (C) when a mixture of air and fuel is pressurized and burned
   - (D) when the fuel has been pressurized

2. Which of the following can be used for inside- and outside-diameter measurements?
   - (A) tape measure
   - (B) outside caliper
   - (C) Vernier caliper
   - (D) level

3. Which valves are open during the power stroke?
   - (A) just the intake valve
   - (B) the intake and exhaust valves
   - (C) just the exhaust valve
   - (D) no valves

4. Which handsaw is used to cut shapes or curves in wood?
   - (A) coping saw
   - (B) band saw
   - (C) cross-cut saw
   - (D) hacksaw

5. What is a tap used for?
   - (A) normal drilling operations
   - (B) removing studs and broken bolts from threaded holes
   - (C) threading holes in metal
   - (D) boring tapered holes in metal

6. The compression stroke occurs when
   - (A) all valves are closed. The piston stroke is from BDC to TDC.
   - (B) all valves are closed. The piston stroke is from TDC to BDC.
   - (C) the intake valve is closed. The exhaust valve is open.
   - (D) the intake valve is open. The exhaust valve is closed.

7. What is the firing order of an engine?
   - (A) intake, compression, power, and exhaust
   - (B) when the valves are opening and closing
   - (C) timed spark in a defined order
   - (D) follows the camshaft rotation

8. Which tool is used with chisels and punches?
   - (A) nail gun
   - (B) ball-peen hammer
   - (C) wooden mallet
   - (D) claw hammer

9. What is exposed to direct heat and pressure during combustion?
   - (A) the cylinder head
   - (B) the piston
   - (C) air
   - (D) fuel

10. Which tool is used to remove a threaded fastener with a head that has a star hole?
    - (A) Security T
    - (B) Torx
    - (C) Robertson
    - (D) Phillips/cross-slot

11. When does the thermostat open?
    - (A) when the engine is cold
    - (B) when the engine is hot
    - (C) during acceleration
    - (D) at start-up

12. Which tool(s) has/have an open-end wrench on one end and a box end on the other?
    - (A) ratchet and socket
    - (B) socket
    - (C) end wrench
    - (D) combination wrench

13. What indicates a defective water pump?
    - (A) an empty coolant recovery bottle
    - (B) the cooling fan not operating
    - (C) coolant leaking out of the water pump weep hole
    - (D) a leaking bypass tube

14. Which screw can be used with a nut and washer combination?
    - (A) sheet metal
    - (B) self-drilling
    - (C) machine
    - (D) wood

15. What does engine lubrication do?
    - (A) cools, cleans, seals, and lubricates parts of the engine
    - (B) carries away heat from the engine
    - (C) helps decrease friction between the exhaust valve and intake valve
    - (D) keeps the cylinder cool during combustion

16. The access panel for a piece of equipment has been placed on the mounting studs. The panel is removed often. Which fastener is used to secure the panel?
    - (A) wing nut
    - (B) bolt
    - (C) lock nut
    - (D) castle nut

17. What do dry sumps use?
    - (A) a premixed oil and fuel ratio
    - (B) an oil tank
    - (C) a fan
    - (D) a thermostat

18. The shop pressed a bearing into a brake rotor assembly. Which fastening device is used to secure the bearing in the rotor bore?
    - (A) inside snap ring
    - (B) outside snap ring
    - (C) internal/external snap-ring pliers
    - (D) locking nut

19. Compression ratios in a diesel engine are
    - (A) lower than gasoline engines.
    - (B) equal to gasoline engines.
    - (C) variable depending on engine sizes.
    - (D) higher than gasoline engines.

20. Which nail is used to attach shingles to a roof board?

(A) finish
(B) framing
(C) drywall
(D) roofing

21. What is the purpose of the fuel pressure regulator?

(A) deliver fuel from the tank to the fuel system
(B) regulate the injector's injection process
(C) regulate fuel pressure in the fuel system for the injectors
(D) adjust the air-fuel ratio

22. What application are rivets used for?

(A) in combination with a jack plane
(B) attaching metal pieces
(C) boring holes in metal
(D) attaching wood pieces

23. A lean mixture is what ratio?

(A) 15:1
(B) 13:1
(C) 14.7:1
(D) 50:50

24. Which welder(s) uses/use a stinger and welding rod to attach metal pieces?

(A) MIG welder
(B) arc welder
(C) oxyacetylene welder
(D) both MIG and arc welder

25. What is pre-ignition?

(A) a part located under the distributor cap
(B) a distributor-less ignition system
(C) when the air-fuel mixture ignites early
(D) when spark happens as the piston reaches BDC

Mechanical Comprehension

This part of the test measures your knowledge of mechanics. Each of the questions or incomplete statements is followed by four choices. You are to decide which one of the choices best answers the question or completes the statement.

1. What is the net force acting on the block below? (Assume positive is to your right.)

   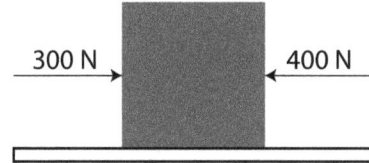

   (A) −100 N
   (B) 0 N
   (C) 700 N
   (D) 120,000 N

2. A person starts from rest and increases his velocity to 5 m/s over a time period of 1 s. What is his acceleration?

   (A) −5 m/s²
   (B) 0 m/s²
   (C) 5 m/s²
   (D) 10 m/s²

3. What is the mechanical advantage of the system of pulleys shown below?

   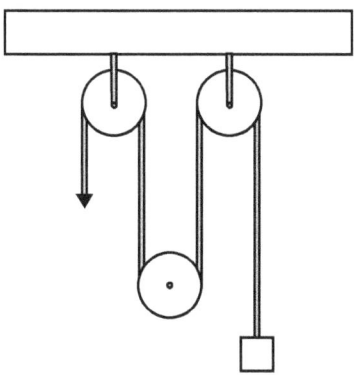

   (A) 0
   (B) 2
   (C) 3
   (D) 6

4. Which of these objects would be the hardest for an astronaut to move in outer space?

   (A) a wrench
   (B) another astronaut
   (C) a screwdriver
   (D) the International Space Station

5. Which of the following terms defines a force?

   (A) a push or pull
   (B) a measure of inertia
   (C) a change in speed
   (D) a change in acceleration

6. If the coefficient of kinetic friction between an object and the floor is $\mu_s = 0.5$, and the weight of the object is 10 N, what is the magnitude of the force of kinetic friction?

   (A) 1 N
   (B) 2 N
   (C) 4 N
   (D) 5 N

7. Which of the following describes what will happen when positive work is done on an object?

   (A) The object will gain energy.
   (B) The object will lose energy.
   (C) The object will increase its temperature.
   (D) The object will decrease its temperature.

PRACTICE TEST ONE

8. What is the potential energy of a person who weighs 150 N when she is on a stool 1 m in the air?
   (A) 15 J
   (B) 30 J
   (C) 150 J
   (D) 300 J

9. A ramp has a length of 20 m, and the top end is rested on a ridge that is 5 m high. What is the mechanical advantage for this ramp?
   (A) 2
   (B) 3
   (C) 4
   (D) 5

10. What is the unit for power?
    (A) watt (W)
    (B) joule (J)
    (C) newton (N)
    (D) coulomb (C)

11. What is the momentum of a mass of 100 kg that is traveling at 2 m/s?
    (A) 50 kg m/s
    (B) 100 kg m/s
    (C) 200 kg m/s
    (D) 400 kg m/s

12. A car wheel has a radius of 1 m and applies a torque of 100 Nm to the road. What is the force applied to the road from the wheel?
    (A) 1 N
    (B) 10 N
    (C) 100 N
    (D) 1,000 N

13. In terms of moment of inertia, which example would be the most difficult for a person to spin in a circle?
    (A) a basketball at half an arm's length
    (B) a bowling ball at half an arm's length
    (C) a basketball at arm's length
    (D) a bowling ball at arm's length

14. What is the best explanation of what a pulley does?
    (A) changes the direction of an input force by supporting a rope that has a tension
    (B) applies an output force with a motor that drives the pulley
    (C) changes the angle of the input force by using an inclined plane
    (D) provides rotational force by friction to increase the output force of the pulley

15. A single pulley is attached to the ceiling. If the pulley is holding a rope that is attached to the floor on one side and a person of weight 100 N on the other, what is the tension in the rope?
    (A) 0 N
    (B) 50 N
    (C) 100 N
    (D) 200 N

16. A screw in a block of wood is rotated exactly once around its axis. What is another name for the distance it moves into the wood?
    (A) impulse
    (B) torque
    (C) wedge
    (D) pitch

17. Two ropes are connected on either side of a mass of 100 kg resting on a flat surface. Each rope is pulling on the mass with 50 N of force, parallel to the ground. What can be said about the motion of the mass?

    (A) The mass will accelerate to left.
    (B) The mass is in equilibrium.
    (C) The mass will accelerate to the right.
    (D) The mass will be lifted up.

18. Two masses each have a mass of 1 kg and are 1 m apart as shown below. Where is the center of mass of the two masses located?

    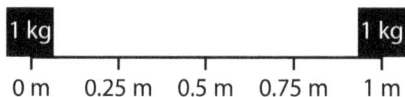

    (A) 0 m
    (B) 0.25 m
    (C) 0.5 m
    (D) 0.75 m

19. Why is it so difficult to hold a beach ball under water?

    (A) The ball is full of air, which is much less dense than water.
    (B) The ball shrinks under water, making it harder to hold.
    (C) The ball expands under water, so it rises faster.
    (D) The cool water will cool the air in the ball, making it rise.

20. How much energy is used by a 60 W light bulb that has been on for 100 s?

    (A) 0.6 J
    (B) 6 J
    (C) 60 J
    (D) 6,000 J

21. In the gear train shown below, Gear B will move _____ and Gear C will move _____.

    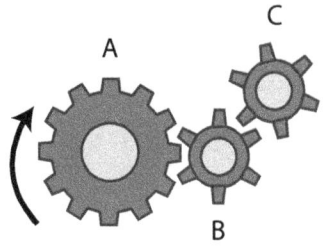

    (A) clockwise; clockwise
    (B) clockwise; counterclockwise
    (C) counterclockwise; counterclockwise
    (D) counterclockwise; clockwise

22. The arrow labeled F in the diagram of a box on an include below represents

    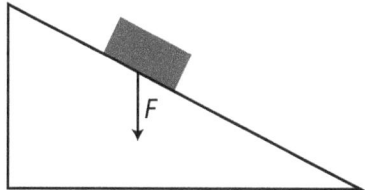

    (A) normal force
    (B) gravity
    (C) friction
    (D) tension

23. Which object will weigh the most?
    (A) an object with mass = 10 kg
    (B) an object with mass = 100 kg
    (C) an object with mass = 1,000 kg
    (D) an object with mass = 10,000 kg

24. Which of the following is a measure of the inertia of an object?
    (A) mass
    (B) speed
    (C) acceleration
    (D) force

25. A pendulum is swinging as shown in the figure below. At which point does the pendulum have the maximum amount of kinetic energy?

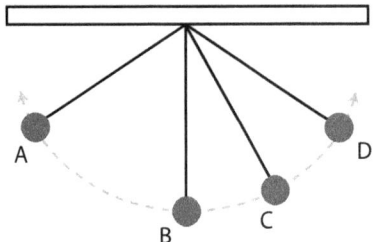

- **(A)** Point A
- **(B)** Point B
- **(C)** Point C
- **(D)** Point D

Assembling Objects

Given a set of objects, your task is to determine which answer choice shows how the objects will look once the parts are put together.

1.
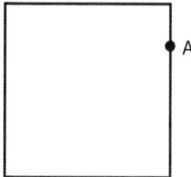

(A)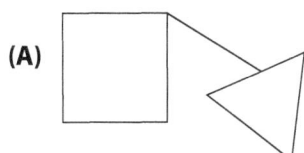

(B)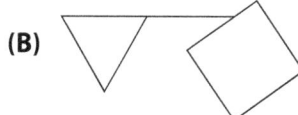

(C)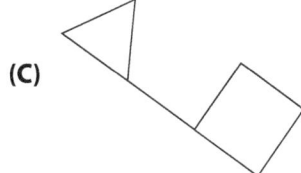

(D)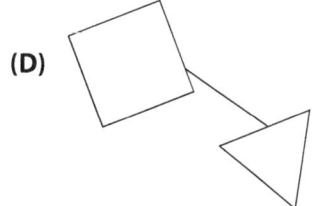

2.
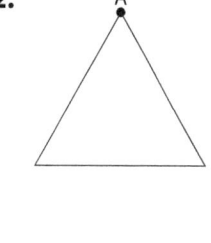
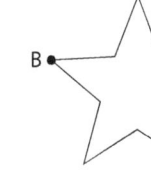

(A)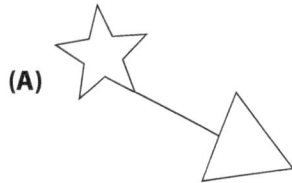

(B)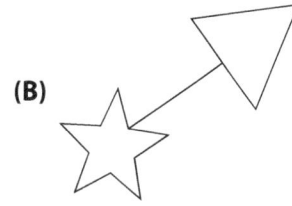

(C)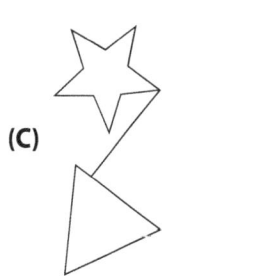

(D)

PRACTICE TEST ONE 29

3.

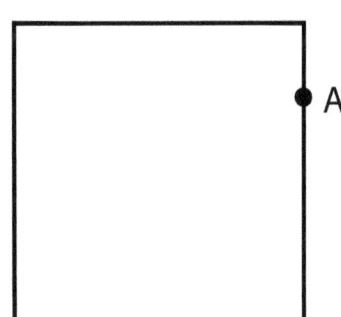

(A)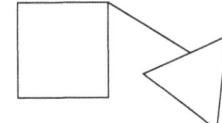

(C)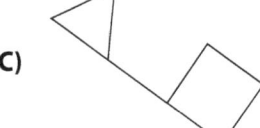

(B)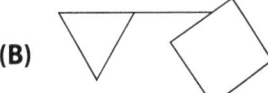

(D)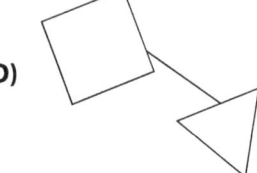

4.

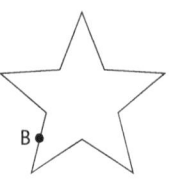

(A)

(C)

(B)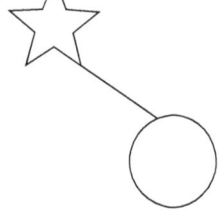

(D)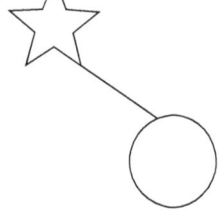

5.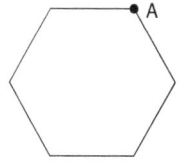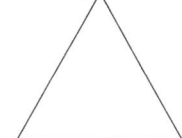

(A)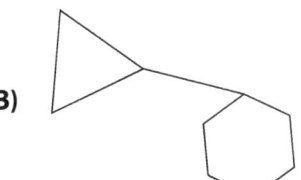

(B)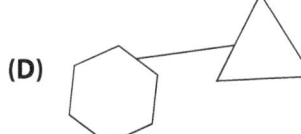

(C)

(D)

6.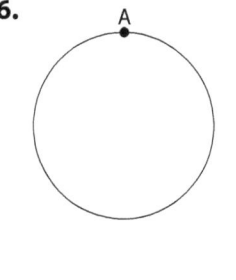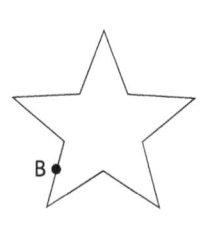

(A)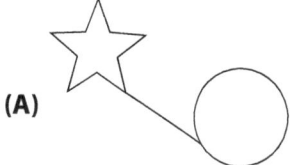

(B)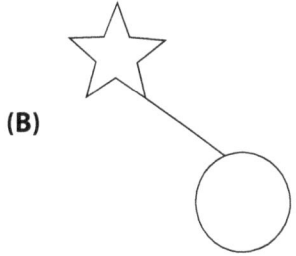

(C)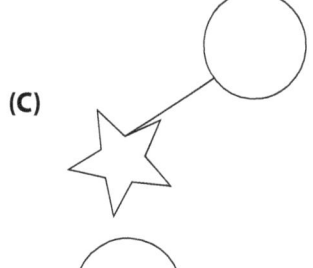

(D)

PRACTICE TEST ONE 31

7.

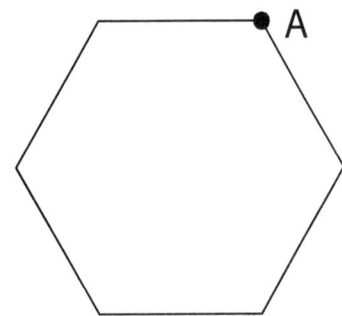

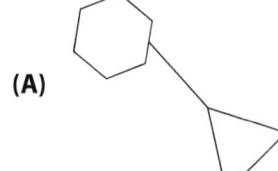
(A)

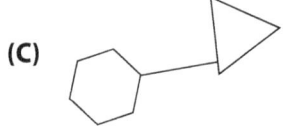
(C)

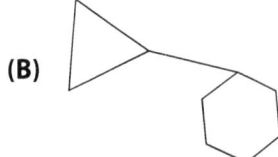
(B)

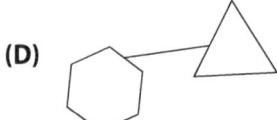
(D)

8.

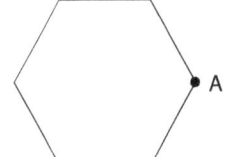

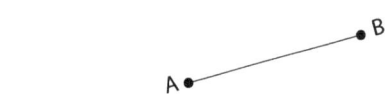

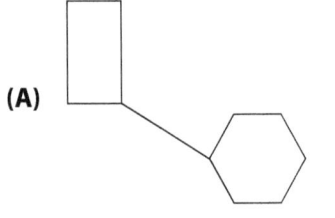
(A)

(C)

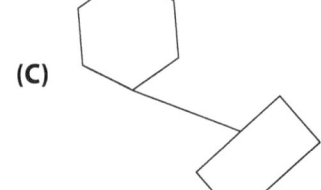

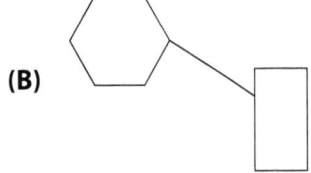
(B)

(D)

9.

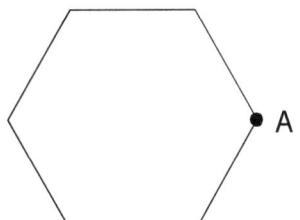

(A)

(C)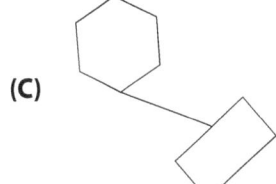

(B)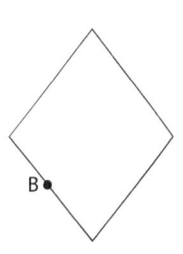

(D)

10.

(A)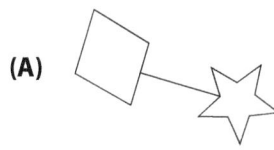

(C)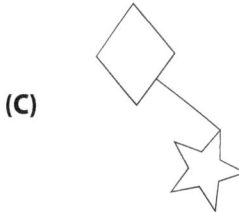

(B)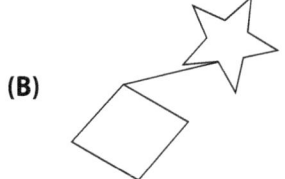

(D)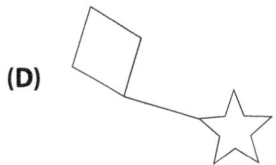

PRACTICE TEST ONE 33

11.

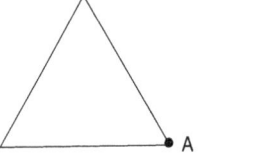

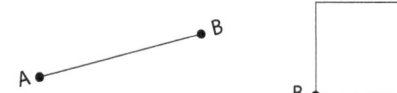

(A)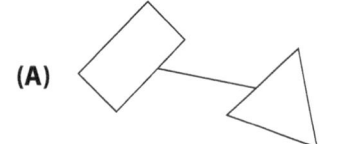

(B)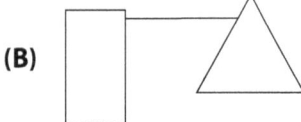

(C)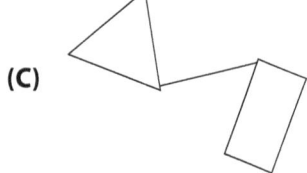

(D)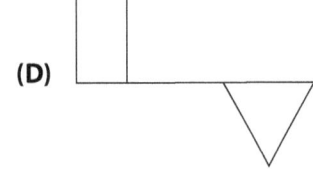

12.

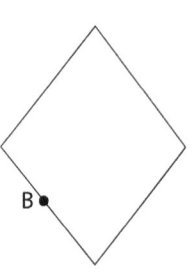

(A)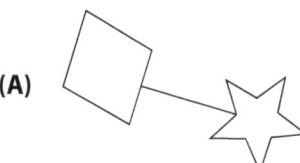

(B)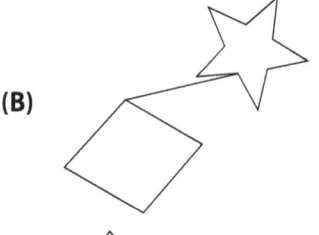

(C)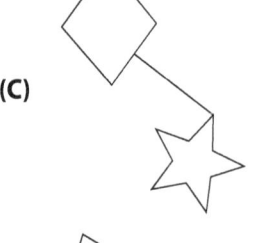

(D)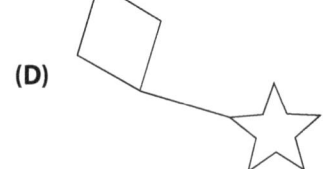

13.

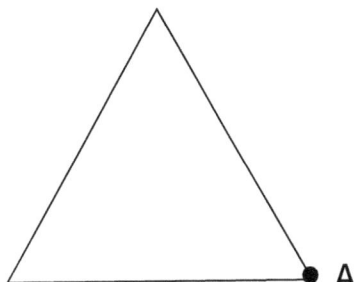

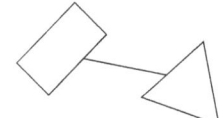 (A)

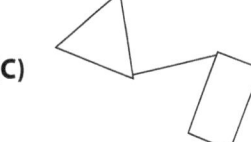 (C)

 (B)

 (D)

14.

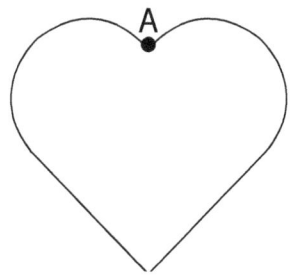

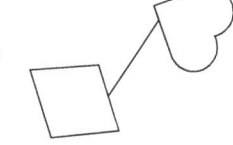 (A)

(C)

 (B)

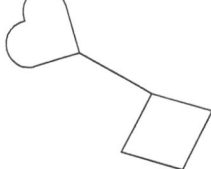 (D)

15.

(A)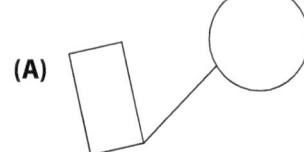

(B)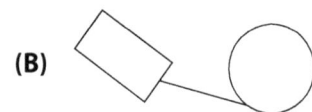

(C)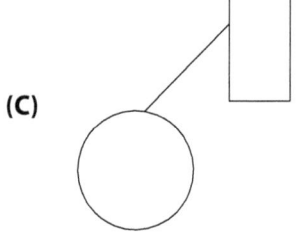

(D)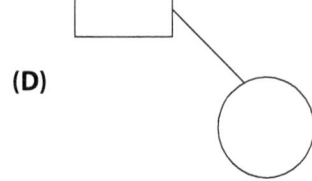

16.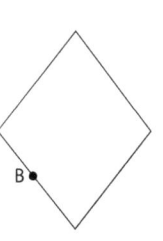

(A)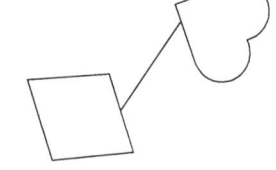

(B)

(C)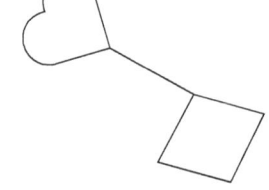

(D)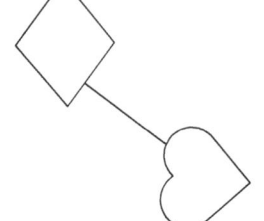

17.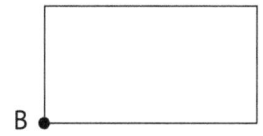

 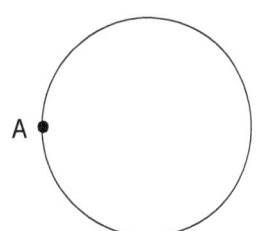

(A)  (C)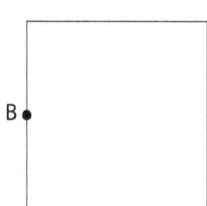

(B) 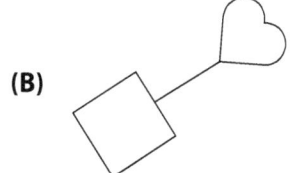 (D)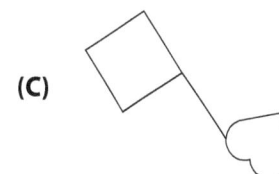

18.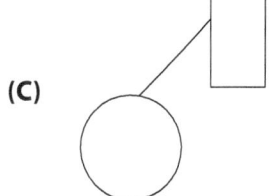

 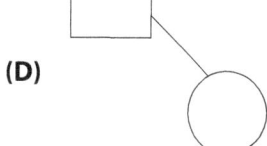

(A) (C)

(B) (D)

PRACTICE TEST ONE 37

19.

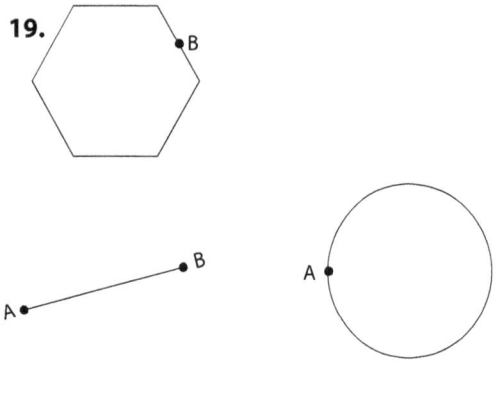

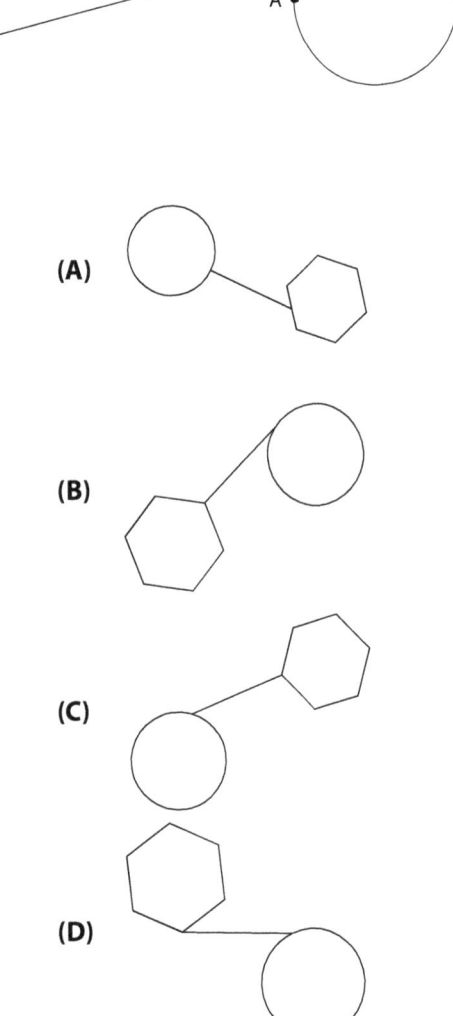

(A)

(B)

(C)

(D)

20.

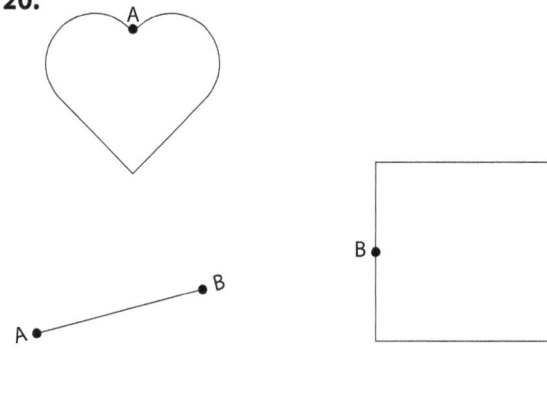

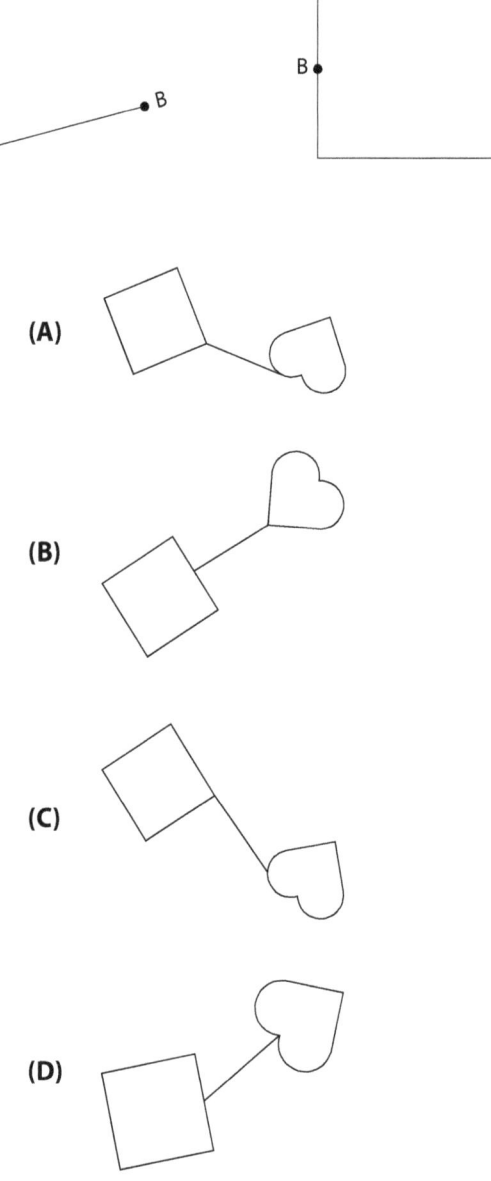

(A)

(B)

(C)

(D)

21.

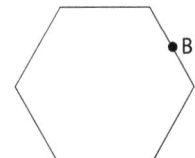

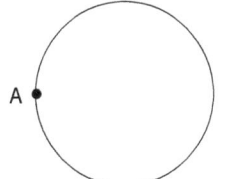

(A)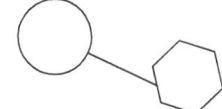
(C)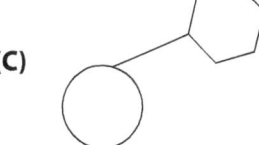

(B)
(D)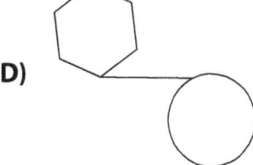

22.

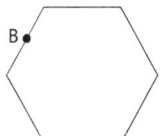

(A)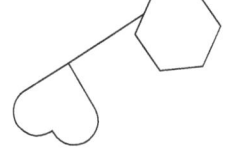
(C)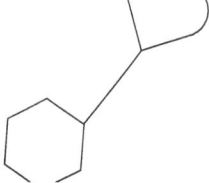

(B)
(D)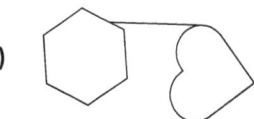

PRACTICE TEST ONE 39

23.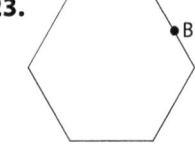

(A)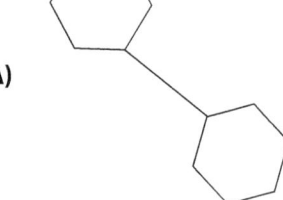

(B)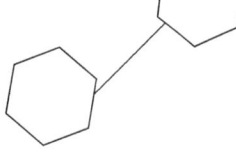

(C)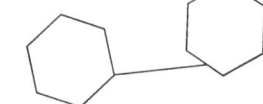

(D)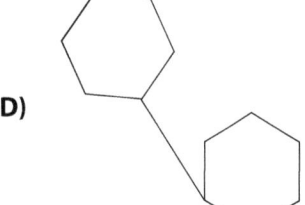

24.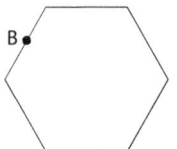

(A)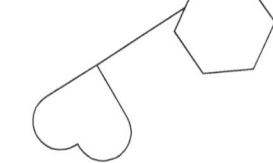

(B)

(C)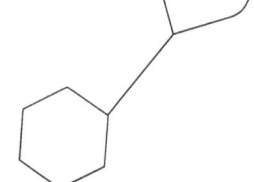

(D)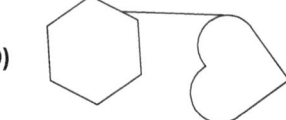

25.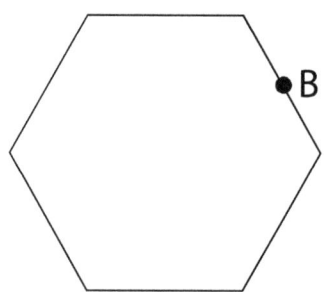

(A)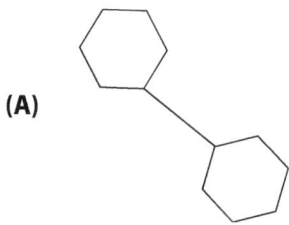

(C)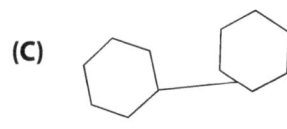

(B)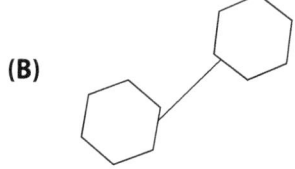

(D)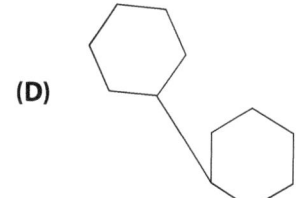

ANSWER KEY

GENERAL SCIENCE

1. **(A)**
   (A) is correct. Calcium is the most abundant mineral found in bones, as well as in the entire body.
   (B) is incorrect. Phosphorus is the second-most common material found in bones.
   (C) is incorrect. Collagen is a protein found in connective tissue.
   (D) is incorrect. Potassium is not found in high quantities in bone.

2. **(A)**
   (A) is correct. A biome is a large ecological community that includes specific plants and animals, such as a desert.
   (B) is incorrect. A cornfield is a part of a prairie biome.
   (C) is incorrect. Animals are part of a biome.
   (D) is incorrect. A beehive is part of a biome.

3. **(B)**
   (A) is incorrect. Mercury is the planet closest to the sun. Venus orbits between Mercury and Earth.
   (B) is correct. Venus's orbit is closest to Earth. Venus is the second planet from the sun, and Earth is the third planet from the sun.
   (C) is incorrect. Jupiter is the fifth planet from the sun.
   (D) is incorrect. Saturn is the sixth planet from the sun.

4. **(D)**
   (A) is incorrect. *Aurora* is the phenomenon of colored lights that appear in the sky near the North and South Poles.
   (B) is incorrect. The galaxy is a large group of stars held together by gravity.
   (C) is incorrect. Black holes are collapsed stars whose gravitational pull is so strong that light cannot escape.
   (D) is correct. Before a star collapses, the star burns brighter for a period of time and then fades from view. This is a supernova.

5. **(D)**
   (A) is incorrect. Mitochondria are not found only in animal cells.
   (B) is incorrect. Mitochondria are not found only in fungi cells.
   (C) is incorrect. Mitochondria are not found only in plant cells.

(D) is correct. Plant, animal, and fungi cells have mitochondria.

6. **(C)**

   (A) is incorrect. Isotopes must have the same number of protons, not electrons.

   (B) is incorrect. Isotopes are defined as having different numbers of neutrons, not the same number.

   (C) is correct. Isotopes are atoms of the same element with the same number of protons but different numbers of neutrons.

   (D) is incorrect. Isotopes have the same number of protons but can also have the same number of electrons.

7. **(D)**

   (A) is incorrect. Blood tests are used to diagnose diabetes.

   (B) is incorrect. Magnetic resonance imaging (MRI) is used to see soft tissue damage, such as torn ligaments.

   (C) is incorrect. There are a variety of tests that diagnose cancer, such as blood tests, magnetic resonance imaging (MRI), and ultrasounds.

   (D) is correct. Tachycardia is an abnormally fast heart rate, and electrocardiograms show the electrical activity of the heart.

8. **(C)**

   (A) is incorrect. Protons are positively charged particles in the nucleus.

   (B) is incorrect. Neutrons are particles in the nucleus that have no charge.

   (C) is correct. Electrons are negatively charged particles in an atom; electrons orbit the nucleus.

   (D) is incorrect. Ions are atoms that have lost or gained electrons and have a charge.

9. **(A)**

   (A) is correct. The metabolic rate of crustaceans is too low to regulate their temperature. Crustaceans use behavioral techniques, such as moving to shallow water, to maintain body temperature.

   (B) is incorrect. Dolphins are mammals. Mammals are endothermic, meaning they have a mechanism to regulate body temperature internally.

   (C) is incorrect. Whales are mammals, and so are endothermic.

   (D) is incorrect. Birds are endothermic.

10. **(A)**

    (A) is correct. Tension is the force that results from objects being pulled or hung.

    (B) is incorrect. The box experiences friction as it slides against the ramp.

    (C) is incorrect. Gravity is the force pulling the box down the ramp.

    (D) is incorrect. The normal force is the upward force of the ramp on the box.

11. **(B)**

    (A) is incorrect. Plants produce their own food through photosynthesis, making them producers.

    (B) is correct. Mushrooms are fungi. Fungi break down organic material left by dead animals and plants, making them decomposers.

    (C) is incorrect. Goats eat producers, such as grass, making them primary consumers.

    (D) is incorrect. Lions are carnivorous animals that feed on primary consumers and secondary consumers, making them secondary or tertiary consumers.

12. **(D)**

    (A) is incorrect. Acids have a pH between 0 and 7.

    (B) is incorrect. Acids have a pH between 0 and 7.

    (C) is incorrect. Acids have a pH between 0 and 7.

    (D) is correct. Bases have a pH between 7 and 14.

13. (B)

(A) is incorrect. The digestive system turns food into energy.

(B) is correct. The endocrine system releases hormones, including growth hormones.

(C) is incorrect. The nervous system is a network of communication cells.

(D) is incorrect. The circulatory system delivers nutrients to cells and removes wastes from the body.

14. (B)

(A) is incorrect. The exosphere is the outermost layer of the earth's atmosphere.

(B) is correct. The lithosphere is the top layer of the earth's surface.

(C) is incorrect. The atmosphere refers to the layer of gases that surrounds the earth.

(D) is incorrect. The biosphere is the part of Earth where life exists; the biosphere includes the atmosphere, the oceans, and the life-supporting areas above and below Earth's surface.

15. (A)

(A) is correct. When water changes form, it does not change the chemical composition of the substance. Once water becomes ice, the ice can easily turn back into water.

(B) is incorrect. During a chemical change, the chemical composition of the substance changes and cannot be reversed. Baking a cake is an example of a chemical change.

(C) is incorrect. Rusting is an example of a chemical change.

(D) is incorrect. Setting off fireworks causes a chemical change.

16. (C)

(A) is incorrect. Water can generate hydropower, which is a renewable energy source.

(B) is incorrect. Wind is a renewable energy source.

(C) is correct. Coal is nonrenewable because once coal is burned, it cannot be quickly replaced.

(D) is incorrect. Solar energy is a renewable energy source.

17. (B)

(A) is incorrect. One hour is 1/24 of the time it takes for the earth to rotate on its axis.

(B) is correct. Earth takes approximately twenty-four hours to rotate on its axis.

(C) is incorrect. The moon takes approximately one month to revolve around the earth.

(D) is incorrect. The earth takes approximately one year to revolve around the sun.

18. (D)

(A) is incorrect. Digestion is the process whereby large food particles are broken down into small particles.

(B) is incorrect. A chloroplast is the part of the cell where photosynthesis takes place.

(C) is incorrect. Decomposition is the process where substances are broken down into smaller parts.

(D) is correct. Photosynthesis describes the process by which plants convert the energy of the sun into stored chemical energy (glucose).

19. (D)

(A) is incorrect. In a substitution reaction, a single atom or ion swaps places with another atom or ion.

(B) is incorrect. In an acid-base reaction, an acid and a base react to neutralize each other. This reaction does not include an acid or base.

(C) is incorrect. In a decomposition reaction, a compound breaks down into smaller molecules or compounds.

(D) is correct. Combustion is defined as a reaction in which a hydrocarbon reacts with O_2 to produce CO_2 and H_2O.

20. (C)

(A) is incorrect. Producers are living things, which are biotic factors.
(B) is incorrect. Consumers are living things.
(C) is correct. Nonliving things in an ecosystem, like air and water, are abiotic factors.
(D) is incorrect. Decomposers are living things.

21. (B)

(A) is incorrect. The respiratory system helps create sound, but that is not its primary purpose.
(B) is correct. Oxygen intake and carbon dioxide disposal are the primary functions of the respiratory system.
(C) is incorrect. The circulatory system transports nutrients throughout the body.
(D) is incorrect. While parts of the respiratory system filter out foreign pathogens, this is not the system's primary purpose.

22. (D)

(A) is incorrect. Gene flow is the transfer of alleles from one population to another.
(B) is incorrect. Genetic drift is the increase or decrease in the presence of an allele due to chance.
(C) is incorrect. A mutation is a change in the genetic code that leads to advantageous traits.
(D) is correct. The mechanism of natural selection is rooted in the idea that there is variation in inherited traits among a population of organisms and that there is differential reproduction as a result.

23. (B)

(A) is incorrect. The pharynx connects the mouth to the esophagus and larynx.
(B) is correct. The tongue is the muscle that helps break apart food, mix it with saliva, and direct it toward the esophagus.
(C) is incorrect. The diaphragm is the muscle that moves the lungs.
(D) is incorrect. The stomach receives the bolus that passes through the esophagus from the mouth.

24. (A)

(A) is correct. Strong acids break apart into their constituent ions immediately when placed in water.
(B) is incorrect. Strong acids may donate only one proton.
(C) is incorrect. A substance with a pH of 7 is neutral; a strong acid has a pH close to 1.
(D) is incorrect. A strong acid ionizes easily, releasing protons.

25. (C)

(A) is incorrect. Cave formation is an example of chemical weathering. Chemical weathering involves a chemical change.
(B) is incorrect. Rusting is an example of chemical weathering.
(C) is correct. Mechanical weathering involves breaking a substance down without changing the composition of the substance.
(D) is incorrect. Bananas turning brown is an example of a chemical change.

ARITHMETIC REASONING

1. **(C)**
   Work backwards to find the number of runners in the competition (*c*) and then the number of runners on the team (*r*).
   $\frac{2}{c} = \frac{10}{100}$
   $c = 20$
   $\frac{20}{r} = \frac{25}{100}$
   r = 80

2. **(D)**
   Multiply by the converstion factor to get from meters to feet.
   $55 \text{ m} \left(\frac{3.28 \text{ ft.}}{1 \text{ m}}\right) =$ **180.4 feet**

3. **(D)**
   Write a proportion and then solve for *x*.
   $\frac{40}{45} = \frac{265}{x}$
   $40x = 11{,}925$
   $x = 298.125 \approx$ **298**

4. **(B)**
   Find the cost of three burgers.
   Cost of 3 burgers = 3(6.50) = 19.50
   Subtract this value from the total costs of the meal to find the cost of the fries.
   26.50 − 19.50 = 7
   Divide by 2 to find the cost of one order of fries.
   7 ÷ 2 = **$3.50**

5. **(B)**
   Write a proportion and then solve for *x*.
   $\frac{15{,}036}{7} = \frac{x}{2}$
   $7x = 30{,}072$
   $x =$ **4,296**

6. **(A)**
   Use the formula for inversely proportional relationships to find *k* and then solve for *s*.
   $sn = k$
   $(65)(250) = k$
   $k = 16{,}250$
   $s(325) = 16{,}250$
   $s =$ **50**

7. **(D)**
   Add the probability of drawing a blue marble and the probability of drawing a red marble to find the probability of drawing either a blue or red marble.
   $\frac{1}{20} + \frac{7}{20} = \frac{8}{20} = \frac{2}{5}$

8. **(C)**
   Use the formula for percent change.
   percent change = $\frac{\text{amount of change}}{\text{original amount}}$
   $= \frac{(7{,}375 - 7{,}250)}{7{,}250} = 0.017 =$ **1.7%**

9. **(A)**
   To calculate the average, add all of the scores and divide by the total number of scores. Use the variable *x* in place of the missing score.
   $\frac{(100 + 100 + 100 + x)}{4} = 85$
   $\frac{(300 + x)}{4} = 85$
   $(300 + x) = 340$
   x = 40%

10. **(A)**
    Add the fractions and subtract the result from the amount of flour Allison started with.
    $2\frac{1}{2} + \frac{3}{4} = \frac{5}{2} + \frac{3}{4} = \frac{10}{4} + \frac{3}{4} = \frac{13}{4}$
    $4 - \frac{13}{4} = \frac{16}{4} - \frac{13}{4} = \frac{3}{4}$

11. **(B)**
    Multiply the number of rooms by the cost of each room to find the total.
    25(4) + 35(2) + 40(1) = **$210**

12. **(A)**

    Use the equation for percentages.
    part = whole × percent =
    9 × 0.25 = **2.25**

13. **(A)**

    Valerie will receive her base pay plus 27.75 for every hour she worked in addition to her 40 hours.
    A = base pay + 27.75 × extra hours
    A = 740 + 27.75(t – 40)

14. **(D)**

    Set up a proportion and solve.
    $\frac{AB}{DE} = \frac{3}{4}$
    $\frac{12}{DE} = \frac{3}{4}$
    3(DE) = 48
    DE = 16

15. **(A)**

    His profit will be his income minus his expenses. He will earn $40 for each lawn, or 40m. He pays $35 is expenses each week, or 35x.
    profit = 40m – 35x

16. **(C)**

    23 ÷ 4 = 5.75 pizzas
    Round up to **6 pizzas**.

17. **(C)**

    Use the formula for percent change.
    percent change = $\frac{amount\ of\ change}{original\ amount}$
    = $\frac{680 - 425}{425}$
    = $\frac{255}{425}$ = 0.60 = **60%**

18. **(C)**

    Use the formula for percentages.
    whole = $\frac{part}{percent} = \frac{meal + tax}{1 + 0.0825}$
    = $\frac{24.65}{1.0825}$ = **$22.77**

19. **(A)**

    Use the formula for percentages to find the number of games the team won.
    part = whole × percent =
    12 × 0.75 = 9

    Subtract the number of games won from the games played to find the number of games the team lost.
    12 – 9 = **3**

20. **(D)**

    Assign variables and write the ratios as fractions. Then, cross-multiply to solve for the number of apples and oranges sold.
    x = apples
    $\frac{apples}{bananas} = \frac{3}{2} = \frac{x}{20}$
    60 = 2x
    x = 30 apples
    y = oranges
    $\frac{oranges}{bananas} = \frac{1}{2} = \frac{y}{20}$
    2y = 20
    y = 10 oranges
    To find the total, add the number of apples, oranges, and bananas together. 30 + 20 + 10 = **60 pieces of fruit**

21. **(D)**

    To estimate the amount of the change, round the price of each item to the nearest dollar amount and subtract from the total.
    $50 – ($13 + $12 + $4 + $6)
    = $50 – $35 = **$15**

22. **(D)**

    Set up an equation to find the number of people wearing neither white nor blue. Subtract the number of people wearing both colors so they are not counted twice.
    21 = 7 + 6 + neither – 5
    neither = **13**

23. **(B)**

    Find the 5th term.
    –9 – (–36) = 27
    27 × –3 = –81
    Find the 6th term.
    –36 – (–81) = 45
    45 × –3 = **–135**

48 Elissa Simon ■ ASVAB Practice Test Book

24. (D)

Use the formula for the area of a rectangle to find the increase in its size.

$A = lw$
$A = (1.4l)(0.6w)$
$A = 0.84lw$

The new area will be 84% of the original area, a decrease of **16%**.

25. (C)

Set up a proportion and solve.

$\frac{2775 \text{ miles}}{3 \text{ hr}} = \frac{x \text{ miles}}{5 \text{ hr}}$

$2775(5) = 3x$

$x = \textbf{4,625 miles}$

26. (D)

Use the formula for the sum of an arithmetic series.

$S_n = \frac{n}{2}(a_1 + a_n)$

$= \frac{n}{2}[2a_1 + (n-1)d]$

$= \frac{180}{2}[2(10) + (180-1)4]$

$= \textbf{66,240 seats}$

27. (D)

Find the time that Erica spends on break and subtract this from her total time at work.

$30 + 2(15) = 1$ hour

$8\frac{1}{2} - 1 = 7\frac{1}{2}$

$= \textbf{7 hours, 30 minutes}$

28. (B)

Multiply the cost per pounds by the number of pounds purchased to find the cost of each fruit.

apples: $2(1.89) = 3.78$
oranges: $1.5(2.19) = 3.285$
$3.78 + 3.285 = 7.065 = \textbf{\$7.07}$

29. (C)

Multiply the car's speed by the time traveled to find the distance.

$1.5(65) = 97.5$ miles
$2.5(50) = 125$ miles
$97.5 + 125 = \textbf{222.5 miles}$

30. (B)

The square root of 169 is **13**.

Word Knowledge

1. **(A)**
   The word root *pax* means "peace," and the suffix *–ify* means "to cause to become more," and so, to pacify someone means to cause that person to become more peaceful, or to soothe him.

2. **(D)**
   The prefix *im–* means "not," and the word root *materialis* means "material, relevant, or important," so *immaterial* means "inconsequential or of no importance."

3. **(B)**
   The root word *flagrantem* means "burning, glowing," and the suffix *–ly* means "having the nature or qualities of." Someone who breaks rules and laws flagrantly does so in an open, deliberate manner, with no shame.

4. **(C)**
   An indolent person is lazy and avoids activity or exertion.

5. **(A)**
   The word root *judicium* means "judgment," and the suffix *–ous* means "possessing or full of." And so, the cat made a decision based on good judgment, wisdom, or practicality.

6. **(C)**
   Pragmatic means "related to practical matters." For example, a pragmatic person evaluates the facts and makes a realistic plan before acting.

7. **(D)**
   Someone with a smiling countenance has a smile on her face.

8. **(A)**
   The word root *kak* means "evil," and the word root *phone* means "sound," so cacophony is the opposite of harmony; it is a combination of harsh, unpleasant noises that sound terrible together.

9. **(D)**
   Someone with charisma, or charm, is attractive to others.

10. **(C)**
    Capricious means "unpredictable or impulsive," so others cannot rely on a capricious person.

11. **(C)**
    To daunt means to intimidate or make someone apprehensive. For example, difficult tests are daunting to most people.

12. **(B)**
    The word root *acclamare* in *acclaim* means "to cry out." Over time, this word came to mean "applause or praise."

13. **(A)**
    The word root *crēdere* means "to believe," and the suffix *–ous* means "possessing or full of," so a credulous person is naïve enough to believe almost everything he hears or reads.

14. **(B)**
    The word root *obsolētus* means "worn out." And so, an obsolete device such as a rotary phone has outlived or worn out its usefulness.

15. **(A)**
    A labyrinth is a maze or intricate pathway. Once someone enters a labyrinth, she can find it very difficult to find the way out.

16. (D)

The word root *sacrōsānctus* means "made holy by sacred rites." Related words include *sacred*, *sacrifice*, *sanction*, and *sanctuary*.

17. (B)

Someone with an effervescent personality is animated, charming, and bubbly. The adjective *effervescent* also means "fizzy," so it can be used to describe a carbonated beverage.

18. (B)

Rudimentary means "basic or elementary." For example, familiarity with the alphabet is a rudimentary reading skill that children learn at a young age.

19. (D)

The word root *fervere* means "to boil." And so, someone who is filled with fervor "boils with" passion or eagerness.

20. (A)

To cajole means to wheedle, coax, or entice someone into doing something. For example, a child might cajole her parents into buying her ice cream.

21. (C)

The prefix *im-* means "not," and the word root *parcial* means "biased," so an impartial jury is one whose members are not biased and are therefore able to evaluate evidence in an objective, unprejudiced manner.

22. (C)

The prefix *im-* means "not," and the word root *mutare* means "to change." And so, a mutation is a change, and something immutable is unchangeable.

23. (B)

Reiterate means "to do something over again." For example, when someone reiterates a piece of information, she restates it.

24. (C)

Bombastic language is too flowery, pretentious, and overly fancy for the topic it describes.

25. (D)

The prefix *pre-* means "before," the word root *cede* means "to go," and the suffix *-ent* means "something that," so a precedent is an event or action that comes before another event or action. A model comes first and is used as a plan to make something else.

26. (A)

Prudent means "wise or judicious." For example, a prudent decision is a wise, practical one.

27. (C)

Haphazard means "a lack of planning or order." For example, when a room is arranged haphazardly, it is disorganized, messy, and chaotic.

28. (C)

The word root *figūrāre* means "to shape," and the suffix *-ive* means "indicating a tendency," so a figurative expression, or figure of speech, is shaped or invented rather than based on literal truth.

29. (C)

Innocuous means "harmless or inoffensive." For example, an innocuous substance is not harmful.

30. (D)

The word root *officium* means "service or duty," and the suffix *-ous* means "possessing or full of." And so, Shelby is someone who perhaps takes her leadership duties so seriously that she acts in an overbearing manner.

31. (C)

The word root *neglegere* means "to neglect," and the suffix root *–ence* means "the act of," so negligence is the act of neglecting—not paying proper attention to—someone or something.

32. (D)

Lax means "loose or open." For example, a lax set of rules would be permissive.

33. (D)

To meander means to wander, roam, or amble around on a winding, twisting route.

34. (D)

The word root in the nouns *arson* and *ardor* means "to burn," and the suffix *–ent* means "doing a certain action," and so an ardent person burns with passion.

35. (C)

To garner things means to gather, acquire, get, or collect them.

Paragraph Comprehension

1. **(A)**

    (A) is correct. The context implies that the fighting was intense and tiring.
    (B) is incorrect. Nothing in the passage addresses the price of the battle.
    (C) is incorrect. The passage indicates nothing about the pattern of fighting.
    (D) is incorrect. The author states that the fighting ultimately led to a US victory.

2. **(B)**

    (A) is incorrect. The author identifies the ideals associated with idealism but does not offer an opinion on or advocate for them.
    (B) is correct. The purpose of the passage is to explain what an idealist believes in. The author does not offer any opinions or try to persuade readers about the importance of certain values.
    (C) is incorrect. The author states that social and political discourse are "permeated with idealism" but does not suggest that this is destructive or wrong.
    (D) is incorrect. The author provides the reader with information but does not seek to change the reader's opinions or behaviors.

3. **(B)**

    (A) is incorrect. The passage states that "vision does not become the dominant sense until around the age of 12 months."
    (B) is correct. The passage states that "infants rely primarily on hearing."
    (C) is incorrect. The sense of touch in not mentioned in the passage.
    (D) is incorrect. The sense of smell is not mentioned in the passage.

4. **(B)**

    (A) is incorrect. While this is stated in the first sentence, it is not the main idea.
    (B) is correct. The passage describes the origin of Yellowstone's geysers.
    (C) is incorrect. While the author states this in the passage, it is not the main idea.
    (D) is incorrect. This is not stated in the passage.

5. **(D)**

    (A) is incorrect. There is no evidence that the protest movement was successful; in fact, the passage implies the opposite.
    (B) is incorrect. While the author states that Western countries observed the events in China, there is no evidence they became involved.
    (C) is incorrect. There is no evidence in the passage that factory workers had any involvement beyond "cheering on" the protestors.
    (D) is correct. The author writes, "it seemed to be the beginning of a political revolution in China, so the world was stunned when, on July 4, Chinese troops and security police stormed the square," stifling any possibility of democratic revolution.

6. **(D)**

    (A) is incorrect. While the text does list several family members of Custer who died in the battle, this is not the main idea.
    (B) is incorrect. The author does not explain why the cavalry was formed.
    (C) is incorrect. The author does not describe the personal relationship between Sitting Bull and Custer.
    (D) is correct. The author writes, "the allied tribes decisively defeated their US foes."

7. **(C)**

(A) is incorrect. The author writes, "scientists uncovered a 3.2 million-year-old non-human hominid they nicknamed 'Lucy.'"

(B) is incorrect. The author does not connect Lucy's discovery with the knowledge about the area's past ecosystem.

(C) is correct. The author writes that before Lucy's discovery, the oldest known fossil from the genus Homo "dated only back to 2.3 million years ago, leaving a 700,000 gap between Lucy's species and the advent of humans."

(D) is incorrect. The author explains it was the 2013 discovery that narrowed the gap.

8. **(D)**

(A) is incorrect. In regional studies, geographers "examine the characteristics of a particular place[.]"

(B) is incorrect. In topical studies, geographers "look at a single physical or human feature that impacts the world[.]"

(C) is incorrect. In physical studies, geographers "focus on the physical features of Earth[.]"

(D) is correct. The passage describes human studies as the study of "the relationship between human activity and the environment," which would include farmers interacting with river systems.

9. **(A)**

(A) is correct. The author writes, "a shoelace knot experiences greater g-force than any rollercoaster can generate," helping the reader understand the strength of the g-force experienced by the knots.

(B) is incorrect. The author does not describe any actual experiments involving rollercoasters.

(C) is incorrect. The author does not assess the findings of the experiment.

(D) is incorrect. The rollercoaster reference is a comparison, not specific evidence.

10. **(B)**

(A) is incorrect. While the author does describe his memory loss, this is not the main idea of the passage.

(B) is correct. The author writes, "From this, scientists learned that different types of memory are handled by different parts of the brain."

(C) is incorrect. The author does explain the differences in long-term and short-term memory formation, but not until the end of the passage.

(D) is incorrect. While it is implied that memories of physical skills are processed differently than memories of events, this is not the main idea of the passage.

11. **(A)**

(A) is correct. The author goes on to describe the shared perspectives of these writers.

(B) is incorrect. The author does not indicate the number of writers.

(C) is incorrect. The author provides no context that implies they were an organized group, simply that they shared certain traits.

(D) is incorrect. The author states that they gathered in one place—Paris.

12. **(D)**

(A) is incorrect. The author writes that the officers, not the volunteers, were veterans.

(B) is incorrect. There passage does not mention a citizenship requirement.

(C) is incorrect. While most of the volunteers were indeed from the Southwest, the passage does not say this was a requirement.

(D) is correct. The author writes, "the army set high standards: all of the recruits had to be skilled on horseback…"

13. **(B)**

(A) is incorrect. The author asserts that, despite the popular narrative, cultural differences were not the cause of the Civil War.

(B) is correct. The author writes, "The Civil War was not a battle of cultural identities—it was a battle about slavery. All other explanations for the war are either a direct consequence of the South's desire for wealth at the expense of her fellow man or a fanciful invention to cover up this sad portion of our nation's history."

(C) is incorrect. The author does not discuss the strengths of the North or provide any reason for why it won the war.

(D) is incorrect. Though the author mentions these cultural beliefs, she does not suggest that these were the reasons the South was defeated.

14. **(B)**

(A) is incorrect. While the author states this, it is not the main idea.

(B) is correct. The author states, "Ignored by the government, an activist group known as Indians of All Tribes sailed to Alcatraz in the early morning hours with eighty-nine men, women, and children." The author goes on to describe the nineteen-month occupation of the island.

(C) is incorrect. The author states that up to 600 people joined the occupation.

(D) is incorrect. The author does not describe any violent action towards protestors.

15. **(D)**

(A) is incorrect. There is no indication that the Bastille was occupied by royalty.

(B) is incorrect. There is no indication that the structure was intended to represent anything.

(C) is incorrect. There is no indication that the Bastille was used for governing.

(D) is correct. The author writes that the Bastille was originally built "to protect the city from English invasion during the Hundred Years' War."

Math Knowledge

1. **(D)**
   Simplify using PEMDAS.
   $z^3(z + 2)^2 - 4z^3 + 2$
   $z^3(z^2 + 4z + 4) - 4z^3 + 2$
   $z^5 + 4z^4 + 4z^3 - 4z^3 + 2$
   $\mathbf{z^5 + 4z^4 + 2}$

2. **(B)**
   Use the rules of exponents to simplify the expression.
   $\frac{(3x^2y^2)^2}{3^3x^{-2}y^3} = \frac{3^2x^4y^4}{3^3x^{-2}y^3} = \frac{x^6y}{3}$

3. **(A)**
   $\left(\frac{1}{2}\right)^3 = \frac{1}{2} \times \frac{1}{2} \times \frac{1}{2} = \frac{1}{8}$

4. **(C)**
   Use the formula for the area of a cylinder.
   $V = \pi r^2 h$
   $= \pi(4^2)(0.5) = \mathbf{25.12 \text{ ft}^3}$

5. **(A)**
   (A) Corresponding angles in right triangles are not necessarily the same, so they do not have to be similar.
   (B) All spheres are similar.
   (C) Corresponding angles in 30-60-90 triangles are the same, so all 30-60-90 triangles are similar.
   (D) Corresponding angles in a square are all the same (90°), so all squares are similar.
   (E) All corresponding angles in cubes are congruent, so they are all similar.

6. **(B)**
   The slope 0.0293 gives the increase in passenger car miles (in billions) for each year that passes. Muliply this value by 5 to find the increase that occurs over 5 years: $5(0.0293) = \mathbf{0.1465 \text{ billion miles}}$.

7. **(A)**
   Simplify each root and add.
   $\sqrt[3]{64} = 4$
   $\sqrt[3]{729} = 9$
   $4 + 9 = \mathbf{13}$

8. **(B)**
   Find the highest possible multiple of 4 that is less than or equal to 397, and then subtract to find the remainder.
   $99 \times 4 = 396$
   $397 - 396 = \mathbf{1}$

9. **(C)**
   Find the height of the cylinder using the equation for surface area.
   $SA = 2\pi rh + 2\pi r^2$
   $48\pi = 2\pi(4)h + 2\pi(4)^2$
   $h = 2$
   Find the volume using the volume equation.
   $V = \pi r^2 h$
   $V = \pi(4)^2(2) = \mathbf{32\pi \text{ ft.}^3}$

10. **(D)**
    Use FOIL to multiply the first two terms.
    $(x + 3)(x - 2) = x^2 + 3x - 2x - 6$
    $= x^2 + x - 6$
    Multiply the resulting trinomial by $(x + 4)$.
    $(x^2 + x - 6)(x + 4) =$
    $x^3 + 4x^2 + x^2 + 4x - 6x - 24$
    $= \mathbf{x^3 + 5x^2 - 2x - 24}$

11. **(C)**
    Plug each value into the equation.
    $4(3 + 4)^2 - 4(3)^2 + 20 = 180 \neq 276$
    $4(4 + 4)^2 - 4(3)^2 + 20 = 240 \neq 276$
    $4(6 + 4)^2 - 4(6)^2 + 20 = \mathbf{276}$
    $4(12 + 4)^2 - 4(12)^2 + 20 = 468 \neq 276$

12. **(A)**
    Plug 0 in for y and solve for x.
    $10x + 10y = 10$
    $10x + 10(0) = 10$
    $x = 1$

The x-intercept is at **(1, 0)**.

13. **(C)**

    Round each value and add.
    129,113 ≈ 129,000
    34,602 ≈ 35,000
    129,000 + 35,000 = **164,000**

14. **(C)**

    Factor the trinomial and set each factor equal to 0.
    $x^2 - 3x - 18 = 0$
    $(x + 3)(x - 6) = 0$
    $(x + 3) = 0$
    x = −3
    $(x - 6) = 0$
    x = 6

15. **(A)**

    Use the midpoint formula to find point B.
    $M_x: \frac{(7 + x)}{2} = -3$
    $x = -13$
    $M_y: \frac{(12 + y)}{2} = 10$
    $y = 8$
    B = **(−13, 8)**

16. **(C)**

    Use the triangle inequality theorem to find the possible values for the third side, then calculate the possible perimeters.
    $13 - 5 < s < 13 + 5$
    $8 < s < 18$
    $13 + 5 + 8 < P < 13 + 5 + 18$
    26 < P < 36

17. **(D)**

    $5 \div 8 = 0.625$
    $0.625 \times 100 = \mathbf{62.5\%}$

18. **(D)**

    Solve the system using substitution.
    $z - 2x = 14 \rightarrow z = 2x + 14$
    $2z - 6x = 18$
    $2(2x + 14) - 6x = 18$
    $4x + 28 - 6x = 18$
    $-2x = -10$
    $x = 5$
    $z - 2(5) = 14$
    z = 24

19. **(D)**

    Plug $m = 3$ and $n = -4$ into the expression and simplify.
    $15m + 2n^2 - 7 =$
    $15(3) + 2(-4)^2 - 7 = \mathbf{70}$

20. **(C)**

    Write out each number to find the largest.
    A. 9299 ones = 9299
    B. 903 tens = 9030
    C. 93 hundreds = **9300**
    D. 9 thousands = 9000
    E. 9 thousandths = 0.009

21. **(A)**

    Use the points to find the slope.
    $m = \frac{y_2 - y_1}{x_2 - x_1} = \frac{-3 - 9}{4 - (-2)} = -2$
    Use the point-slope equation to find the equation of the line.
    $(y - y_1) = m(x - x_1)$
    $y - (-3) = -2(x - 4)$
    y = −2x + 5

22. **(D)**

    All the points lie on the circle, so each line segment is a radius. The sum of the 4 lines will be 4 times the radius.
    $r = \frac{75}{2} = 37.5$
    $4r = \mathbf{150}$

23. **(B)**

    Add 5 to each side to isolate the variable k.
    $10 \leq k - 5$
    $15 \leq k$
    k ≥ 15

24. **(B)**

    Calculate the volume of water in tank A.
    $V = l \times w \times h$

$5 \times 10 \times 1 = 50 \text{ ft}^3$

Find the height this volume would reach in tank B.

$V = l \times w \times h$
$50 = 5 \times 5 \times h$
$h = \textbf{2 ft}$

25. **(B)**

Plug each set of values into the inequality $2a - 5b > 12$ and simplify.

(A) $2(2) - 5(6) = -26 \not> 12$
(B) $2(1) - 5(-3) = \textbf{17} > \textbf{12}$
(C) $2(-1) - 5(3) = -17 \not> 12$
(D) $2(7) - 5(2) = 4 \not> 12$

Electronics

1. **(C)**

   (A) is incorrect. An atom with a charge of −17e would have seventeen more electrons than protons.

   (B) is incorrect. An atom with a charge of −7e would have seven more electrons than protons.

   (C) is correct. This atom has a total charge of −5e + 12e = +7e.

   (D) is incorrect. An atom with a charge of +17 would have seventeen more protons than electrons.

2. **(A)**

   (A) is correct. Watts (W) is the unit for power.

   (B) is incorrect. Amperes (A) is the unit for current.

   (C) is incorrect. Joules (J) is the unit for energy.

   (D) is incorrect. Ohms (Ω) is the unit for resistance.

3. **(D)**

   (A) is incorrect. Positive and negative charge is neither created nor destroyed. No particle can change its charge.

   (B) is incorrect. Electrons, not protons, move to create current.

   (C) is incorrect. Voltage sources are sources of electric potential. They do not store electrons.

   (D) is correct. The valence electrons are the outermost and most loosely held electrons. They are more likely to move in a conducting material.

4. **(B)**

   (A) is incorrect. Conventional current is in the opposite direction of the flow of electrons.

   (B) is correct. Conventional current is in the same direction of the flow of holes.

   (C) is incorrect. Direct current means current has a constant value.

   (D) is incorrect. Alternating current means current alternates direction.

5. **(B)**

   Use Ohm's law.
   $V = IR = (5 A)(0.5 \Omega) =$ **2.5 V**

6. **(D)**

   (A) is incorrect. All power supplies have an EMF.

   (B) is incorrect. Mechanical movement provides EMF in an electric generator.

   (C) is incorrect. A changing magnetic field creates EMF in a generator, inductor, or transformer.

   (D) is correct. Chemical reactions create the EMF in batteries.

7. **(A)**

   (A) is correct. It is usually easy to see if the wire is intact or if it has been destroyed from a blown fuse.

   (B) is incorrect. A blown fuse is an open circuit with infinite resistance.

   (C) is incorrect. This describes a circuit breaker.

   (D) is incorrect. This behavior would occur in a current limiter circuit.

8. **(B)**

   (A) is incorrect. The symbol for a diode is:

   (B) is correct. This is the figure for a switch.

   (C) is incorrect. The symbol for a fuse is: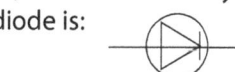

   (D) is incorrect. The symbol for a battery is:

9. **(D)**

   Use Ohm's law.
   $R = \frac{V}{I} = \frac{10 V}{0.005 A} = 2{,}000 \, \Omega =$ **2 kΩ**

10. **(A)**

 Use the equation for equivalent resistance in a parallel circuit.
 $$\frac{1}{R_{eq}} = \frac{1}{R_1} + \frac{1}{R_2} + \ldots + \frac{1}{R_n}$$
 $$\frac{1}{R_{eq}} = \frac{1}{1\,k\Omega} + \frac{1}{2\,k\Omega} + \frac{1}{0.5\,k\Omega} = 3.5\frac{1}{k\Omega}$$
 $$\frac{1}{R_{eq}} = \mathbf{0.3\,k\Omega}$$

11. **(A)**

 (A) is correct. A dimmer needs a variable resistance to raise and lower the amount of voltage and therefore the current through the light bulb.

 (B) is incorrect. A regular light switch is simply off and on.

 (C) is incorrect. A doorbell button is similar to a switch. No variable resistance is needed.

 (D) is incorrect. A key on a keyboard is similar to a switch. No variable resistance is needed.

12. **(B)**

 (A) is incorrect. The capacitor does not act as a switch.

 (B) is correct. The capacitor stores energy in the electric field.

 (C) is incorrect. The diode allows current in only one direction.

 (D) is incorrect. The heating element in an oven is a resistor.

13. **(A)**

 (A) is correct. The most common use of a transistor is as a switch.

 (B) is incorrect. The transistor cannot be used as a capacitor.

 (C) is incorrect. The transistor cannot be used as a solenoid.

 (D) is incorrect. The transistor cannot be used as a laser.

14. **(C)**

 (A) is incorrect. A transformer would be used in this application.

 (B) is incorrect. A transformer would be used in this application.

 (C) is correct. A rectifier changes AC into DC.

 (D) is incorrect. And inverter changes DC into AC.

15. **(C)**

 (A) is incorrect. The inductor does not act as an antenna.

 (B) is incorrect. Sound is made from vibrations, and the inductor should not vibrate.

 (C) is correct. The inductor resists current change due to its self-inductance.

 (D) is incorrect. A rectifier converts AC into DC.

16. **(A)**

 (A) is correct. Because the power supply and the rotation are at the same frequency, this is a synchronous motor.

 (B) is incorrect. An asynchronous motor has different rotation and input power frequencies.

 (C) is incorrect. The speed of the motor is not provided in the question.

 (D) is incorrect. The torque of the motor is not provided in the question.

17. **(A)**

 (A) is correct. The stator field is the magnetic field produced in the stator assembly.

 (B) is incorrect. The stator field is a magnetic field.

 (C) is incorrect. The stator field is the magnetic field produced in the stator assembly.

 (D) is incorrect. The stator field is a magnetic field created in the stator.

18. **(B)**

 (A) is incorrect. An alternator produces AC power.

 (B) is correct. A transformer converts voltages to different values.

 (C) is incorrect. A rectifier converts AC to DC.

(D) is incorrect. A capacitor is an energy storage element in electronic circuits.

19. **(C)**

    Use Ohm's law.
    $I = \frac{V}{R} = \frac{120 \text{ V}}{15 \text{ }\Omega} =$ **8 A**

20. **(D)**

    (A) is incorrect. Capacitors store energy in an electric field.

    (B) is incorrect. Batteries store chemical energy.

    (C) is incorrect. Inductors store energy in a magnetic field.

    (D) is correct. A transformer uses electromagnetic induction to transfer electrical energy between two circuits.

Automotive and Shop Information

1. **(C)**
   (A) is incorrect. An air-fuel mixture must enter the cylinder, then be compressed and then ignited.
   (B) is incorrect. The air-fuel mixture must be heated.
   (C) is correct. Combustion is the process of a controlled explosion from a burning pressurized air-fuel mixture.
   (D) is incorrect. The air-fuel mixture needs to be pressurized then burnt—ignited.

2. **(C)**
   (A) is incorrect. A tape measure is used for linear measurements in construction.
   (B) is incorrect. An outside caliper is used only for outside measurements.
   (C) is correct. A Vernier caliper is used for both inside and outside measurements.
   (D) is incorrect. A level is used to check the level of machinery and framework.

3. **(D)**
   (A) is incorrect. Intake is closed at this time.
   (B) is incorrect. Both are closed at this time.
   (C) is incorrect. Exhaust is closed at this time.
   (D) is correct. Both valves need to be closed for the power stroke to happen.

4. **(A)**
   (A) is correct. A coping saw is used to cut shapes or curves into wood.
   (B) is incorrect. A band saw is not a handsaw. With the appropriate blade, it can cut metal.
   (C) is incorrect. This saw is used to cut against the grain on wooden boards.
   (D) is incorrect. A hacksaw is used to cut metal.

5. **(C)**
   (A) is incorrect. Right-hand bits are used for normal drilling operations.
   (B) is incorrect. Left-hand bits rotate counterclockwise to turn the object out of the threads.
   (C) is correct. A tap is used to thread holes.
   (D) is incorrect. A tap can only thread holes.

6. **(A)**
   (A) is correct. The compression stroke occurs when all valves are closed, and the piston is moving from BDC to TDC to compress the air-fuel mixture.
   (B) is incorrect. This is the power stroke.
   (C) is incorrect. This is the exhaust stroke.
   (D) is incorrect. This is the intake stroke.

7. **(C)**
   (A) is incorrect. This is the four-cycle process.
   (B) is incorrect. This allows intake air and exhaust to leave.
   (C) is correct. The spark firing is in a defined order: cylinder 1, then 3, then 4, and finally 2.
   (D) is incorrect. Camshaft rotation is part of timing.

8. **(B)**
   (A) is incorrect. A nail gun will only drive nails.
   (B) is correct. A ball-peen hammer is used with chisels.
   (C) is incorrect. A wooden mallet is not used with impact tools.
   (D) is incorrect. A claw hammer is used to drive and remove nails.

9. **(B)**
   (A) is incorrect. The cylinder head helps contain the heat and pressure.

(B) is correct. The piston head is exposed.
(C) is incorrect. Air is part of the combustion, but fuel is needed too.
(D) is incorrect. Fuel is part of the combustion, but air is needed too.

10. **(B)**
(A) is incorrect. This fastener has a star hole and rod insert in the head.
(B) is correct. A Torx fastener has a star hole in head.
(C) is incorrect. A Robertson fastener does not have a star hole in the head.
(D) is incorrect. This fastener does not have a star hole in the head.

11. **(B)**
(A) is incorrect. The thermostat is closed at this time.
(B) is correct. The thermostat opens when the engine is hot.
(C) is incorrect. Acceleration does not have anything to do with the thermostat opening or closing.
(D) is incorrect. The thermostat should be closed at start-up. The engine would be cold.

12. **(D)**
(A) is incorrect. Neither a ratchet nor a socket is a wrench.
(B) is incorrect. A ratchet must be used with a socket.
(C) is incorrect. An end wrench does not have a box end.
(D) is correct. A combination wrench has both an open end and a box end.

13. **(C)**
(A) is incorrect. This would be a sign of a major leak in the system.
(B) is incorrect. If the fan was not working, this would indicate another component has failed.
(C) is correct. A weep hole is used to show signs of damaged seals or bearings.
(D) is incorrect. If the bypass tube is leaking, it is either disconnected or cracked.

14. **(C)**
(A) is incorrect. This screw is used for attaching sheet metal to framework.
(B) is incorrect. A self-drilling screw is used for metal and does not need a pilot hole.
(C) is correct. A machine screw is used with a washer and nut combination or with a threaded hole.
(D) is incorrect. This screw is used for wood applications only.

15. **(A)**
(A) is correct. Engine lubrication has these four functions.
(B) is incorrect. Coolant does this.
(C) is incorrect. The valves should never touch.
(D) is incorrect. Coolant or air help remove heat from the cylinder.

16. **(A)**
(A) is correct. Wing nuts are designed to be removed quickly and often.
(B) is incorrect. Standard bolts are designed for permanent installations. Bolts cannot be used with studs.
(C) is incorrect. Lock nuts are designed for permanent installations.
(D) is incorrect. A castle nut is used with a cotter key and is often used in front-end applications.

17. **(B)**
(A) is incorrect. This is used in two-stroke engines.
(B) is correct. Dry sumps use an oil tank to store oil.
(C) is incorrect. This is part of the cooling system.
(D) is incorrect. This is part of the cooling system.

18. **(A)**
(A) is correct. An inside snap ring is used to secure bearings inside a bore.
(B) is incorrect. This is used to secure a bearing to a shaft.

(C) is incorrect. Snap-ring pliers are used to install and remove snap rings.
(D) is incorrect. Locking nuts are on studs or bolts.

19. **(D)**
(A) is incorrect. The compression in a diesel engine is higher than a gasoline engine.
(B) is incorrect. The compression in a diesel engine is higher than a gasoline engine.
(C) is incorrect. The compression in a diesel engine is higher than a gasoline engine.
(D) is correct. The compression in a diesel engine is higher than a gasoline engine.

20. **(D)**
(A) is incorrect. These nails are used in furniture applications.
(B) is incorrect. Framing nails are used to attach boards in construction applications.
(C) is incorrect. These nails are used to attach drywall to wood framing.
(D) is correct. Roofing nails are used to attach shingles to roof boarding.

21. **(C)**
(A) is incorrect. The fuel pump delivers fuel to the fuel system.
(B) is incorrect. Normally a control module will regulate when the injector sprays. Older mechanical systems vary.
(C) is correct. The pressure regulator regulates the fuel pressure to the injectors.
(D) is incorrect. The control module and other components help adjust the air-fuel ratio.

22. **(B)**
(A) is incorrect. A jack plane is used for wood-finishing operations.
(B) is correct. Rivets are used for connecting pieces of metal.
(C) is incorrect. Drill bits bore holes.
(D) is incorrect. Wood screws are used for wood applications.

23. **(A)**
(A) is correct. A lean mixture is 15:1.
(B) is incorrect. This is a rich mixture.
(C) is incorrect. This mixture is optimal for an air-fuel ratio.
(D) is incorrect. This is normally a coolant mixture.

24. **(B)**
(A) is incorrect. A MIG welder uses wire feed.
(B) is correct. An arc welder uses a welding rod.
(C) is incorrect. An oxyacetylene welder uses a fill rod.
(D) is incorrect. A is the only correct answer.

25. **(C)**
(A) is incorrect. Pre-ignition is a symptom, not a part.
(B) is incorrect. Pre-ignition is a symptom, not a part.
(C) is correct. Pre-ignition is when the piston is traveling upward, but the air-fuel mixture ignites before the piston reaches TDC.
(D) is incorrect. Pre-ignition normally happens at TDC.

Mechanical Comprehension

1. **(A)**

    Sum the forces to find the net force on the block.
    $F_r - F_l = 300 - 400 \text{ N} = \mathbf{-100 \text{ N}}$

2. **(C)**

    Use the formula for acceleration.
    $a = \frac{\Delta v}{t} = \frac{5 - 0 \text{ m/s}}{1 \text{ s}} = \mathbf{5 \text{ m/s}^2}$

3. **(C)**

    The mechanical advantage for a system of pulleys is equal to the number of pulleys. The MA of the system shown is **3**.

4. **(D)**

    (A) is incorrect. A wrench has a small mass compared to the International Space Station, so it would be easier to move.

    (B) is incorrect. While another astronaut has a larger mass than the tools in the other answer choices, a human being is still quite small in mass compared to the International Space Station. This option is incorrect.

    (C) is incorrect. A screwdriver has a small mass compared to the International Space Station, so it would be easier to move.

    (D) is correct. The largest mass will be the hardest to move. The space station has the largest mass.

5. **(A)**

    (A) is correct. This is the proper definition.

    (B) is incorrect. This describes mass.

    (C) is incorrect. This describes the magnitude of the acceleration.

    (D) is incorrect. This defines the term *jerk*.

6. **(D)**

    Use the equation for kinetic friction. In this case, the normal force will equal the weight of the object.
    $f_k = \mu_k N$
    $f_k = 0.5 \times 10 \text{ N} = \mathbf{5 \text{ N}}$

7. **(A)**

    (A) is correct. The object will gain energy.

    (B) is incorrect. The object will lose energy if negative work is done.

    (C) is incorrect. It is not guaranteed that the temperature will change.

    (D) is incorrect. It is not guaranteed that the temperature will change.

8. **(C)**

    Use the formula for potential energy.
    $PE = Wh = (150 \text{ N})(1 \text{ m}) = \mathbf{150 \text{ J}}$

9. **(C)**

    Use the formula for mechanical advantage of a ramp.
    $MA = \frac{L}{h} = \frac{20}{5} = \mathbf{4}$

10. **(A)**

    (A) is correct. Power is measured in watts (W).

    (B) is incorrect. Energy is measured in joules (J).

    (C) is incorrect. Force is measured in newtons (N).

    (D) is incorrect. Electric charge is measured in coulombs (C).

11. **(C)**

    Use the formula for momentum.
    $p = mv = (100 \text{ kg})(2 \text{ m/s})$
    $= \mathbf{200 \text{ kg m/s}}$

12. **(C)**

    Use the formula for torque.
    $\tau = rF$
    $F = \frac{\tau}{r} = \frac{100 \text{ Nm}}{1 \text{ m}} = \mathbf{100 \text{ N}}$

13. **(D)**

    The moment of inertia is largest when the mass is large and the distance of the mass from the axis of rotation is large.

14. **(A)**

    (A) is correct. This is the correct explanation of the operation of a pulley.
    (B) is incorrect. A pulley does not have a motor.
    (C) is incorrect. A pulley does not have an inclined plane.
    (D) is incorrect. A torque from friction will lower the effectiveness of the pulley.

15. **(C)**

    The tension will be equal to the weight it supports, **100 N**.

16. **(D)**

    (A) is incorrect. Impulse is *force × time*.
    (B) is incorrect. Torque is rotational force.
    (C) is incorrect. A wedge is a simple machine.
    (D) is correct. Pitch is the distance a screw goes into the wood during one rotation.

17. **(B)**

    (A) is incorrect. The net force on the object will be zero; there is no acceleration.
    (B) is correct. The net force on the object will be zero, so the mass is in equilibrium.
    (C) is incorrect. The net force on the object will be zero; there is no acceleration.
    (D) is incorrect. There is no component of the applied forces in the vertical direction.

18. **(C)**

    Use the formula for center of mass.
    $$x_{cm} = \frac{m_1 x_1 + m_2 x_2}{m_1 + m_2} = \frac{0 + (1 \text{ kg})(1 \text{ m})}{1 \text{ kg} + 1 \text{ kg}}$$
    $$= \mathbf{0.5 \text{ m}}$$

19. **(A)**

    (A) is correct. The weight of the air in the ball is much less than the same volume of water that was displaced. Therefore, the buoyant upward force is very large.
    (B) is incorrect. It was not stated that the ball shrinks, and the ball would still feel a large buoyant force upward.
    (C) is incorrect. It was not stated that the ball expands, and the ball would still feel a large buoyant force upward.
    (D) is incorrect. It will have a large buoyant force regardless of the temperature.

20. **(D)**

    Use the formula for power.
    $P = \frac{E}{t}$
    $E = Pt = (60 \text{ W})(100 \text{ s}) = \mathbf{6{,}000 \text{ J}}$

21. **(D)**

    Each gear will move in the opposite direction as the gear driving its motion. Because Gear A is moving clockwise, Gear B will move counterclockwise. Gear C will then move clockwise.

22. **(B)**

    (A) is incorrect. The normal force will be perpendicular to the surface of the incline and will point up.
    (B) is correct. The arrow *F* represents gravity, which is pulling the box down toward the Earth.
    (C) is incorrect. Friction would point parallel to the surface of the incline in a direction opposite to the box's motion.
    (D) is incorrect. Tension is created by hanging objects, which do not appear in the diagram.

23. (D)

Weight is directly proportional to mass ($W = mg$), so the largest mass will have the largest weight.

24. (A)

(A) is correct. Mass is a measure of an object's inertia.
(B) is incorrect. Speed is distance over time.
(C) is incorrect. Acceleration is the change of velocity over time.
(D) is incorrect. A force is a push or pull.

25. (B)

(A) is incorrect. As it nears its highest point, the pendulum will have a large amount of potential energy and almost no kinetic energy.
(B) is correct. At the bottom of its swing, the pendulum will have its maximum amount of kinetic energy and no potential energy.
(C) is incorrect. Midway through its swing, the pendulum will have a mix of kinetic and potential energy.
(D) is incorrect. As it nears its highest point, the pendulum will have a large amount of potential energy and almost no kinetic energy.

ASSEMBLING OBJECTS

1. (B)
2. (D)
3. (A)
4. (C)
5. (B)
6. (D)
7. (C)
8. (A)
9. (D)
10. (D)
11. (D)
12. (C)
13. (A)
14. (A)
15. (A)
16. (B)
17. (C)
18. (B)
19. (A)
20. (D)
21. (D)
22. (B)
23. (C)
24. (A)
25. (C)

PRACTICE TEST TWO

GENERAL SCIENCE

This part of the test measures your knowledge in the area of science. Each of the questions or incomplete statements is followed by four choices. You are to decide which one of the choices best answers the question or completes the statement.

1. Which of the following is NOT a hormone-producing gland of the endocrine system?
   (A) kidneys
   (B) hypothalamus
   (C) testes
   (D) thyroid

2. Which organelle makes proteins?
   (A) mitochondria
   (B) cytoplasm
   (C) vacuoles
   (D) ribosomes

3. Which statement about the solar system is true?
   (A) Earth is much closer to the sun than it is to other stars.
   (B) The moon is closer to Venus than it is to Earth.
   (C) At certain times of the year, Jupiter is closer to the sun than Earth is.
   (D) Mercury is the closest planet to Earth.

4. What term describes a long-term relationship between two species in which one species benefits, to the detriment of the other species?
   (A) mutualism
   (B) parasitism
   (C) commensalism
   (D) predation

5. In which part of a plant does photosynthesis take place?
   (A) the roots
   (B) the stem
   (C) the bark
   (D) the flower

6. Which of the following is caused by geothermal heat?
   (A) geysers
   (B) glaciers
   (C) tsunamis
   (D) tornadoes

7. Which statement about mass and weight is true?
   (A) Mass and weight always have the same value.
   (B) Mass is created by gravitational pull.
   (C) Weight is created by gravitational pull.
   (D) Mass is related to the surface area of an object.

8. The exchange of gases happens in which parts of the respiratory system?
   (A) alveoli
   (B) brochi
   (C) lobes
   (D) trachea

9. When Earth moves between the moon and the sun, it is called a(n)
   (A) solar eclipse.
   (B) lunar eclipse.
   (C) black hole.
   (D) supernova.

10. Enzymes are an example of which type of macromolecule?
    (A) lipids
    (B) DNA
    (C) RNA
    (D) proteins

11. Which gas is produced by burning fossil fuels?
    (A) helium
    (B) oxygen
    (C) nitrogen
    (D) carbon dioxide

12. A warm air mass moving into a cold air mass is called a
    (A) warm front.
    (B) cold front.
    (C) isobar.
    (D) tornado.

13. Which of the following is NOT a cause of extinction?
    (A) invasive species
    (B) climate change
    (C) habitat conservation
    (D) overexploitation by humans

14. What is the part of a neuron that sends electrical signals away from the neuron cell?
    (A) axon
    (B) dendrite
    (C) stimulus
    (D) myelin sheath

15. Which substance is a good thermal conductor?
    (A) plastic
    (B) rubber
    (C) porcelain
    (D) aluminum

16. Which example demonstrates body systems working together to maintain homeostasis?
    (A) Jessica's tracheotomy opened a breathing obstruction.
    (B) Max's muscles, tendons, and ligaments allow his joints to bend.
    (C) Kevin's bones thicken from an excessive production of growth hormones.
    (D) Stacy shivers from the cold.

17. A microscope makes use of which property of waves to make objects appear larger?
    (A) wavelength
    (B) diffraction
    (C) amplitude
    (D) refraction

18. Which planet does NOT have a moon?
    - (A) Mercury
    - (B) Earth
    - (C) Jupiter
    - (D) Saturn

19. Which organism is a reptile?
    - (A) crocodile
    - (B) frog
    - (C) salamander
    - (D) salmon

20. Which of the following is NOT a nucleotide of DNA?
    - (A) adenine
    - (B) guanine
    - (C) thymine
    - (D) uracil

21. Which of the following is a heterogeneous mixture?
    - (A) soil
    - (B) salt water
    - (C) steel
    - (D) air

22. Which measurement describes the distance between crests in a wave?
    - (A) amplitude
    - (B) wavelength
    - (C) frequency
    - (D) period

23. Which trait defines a saturated solution?
    - (A) The solute and solvent are not chemically bonded.
    - (B) Both the solute and solvent are liquid.
    - (C) The solute is distributed evenly throughout the solution.
    - (D) No more solute can be dissolved in the solution.

24. What position do most fungi occupy in a food web?
    - (A) producers
    - (B) primary consumers
    - (C) secondary consumers
    - (D) decomposers

25. Mitosis produces two daughter cells that each have _____ number of chromosomes in the parent cell.
    - (A) a quarter of the
    - (B) half of the
    - (C) the same
    - (D) double the

Arithmetic Reasoning

This part of the test measures your ability to use arithmetic to solve problems. Each problem is followed by four possible answers. You are to decide which one of the four choices is correct.

1. 85 percent of the senior class at a high school will be graduating. If the class has 540 students, how many students will graduate?
   - (A) 448
   - (B) 452
   - (C) 453
   - (D) 459

2. In a theater, there are 4,500 lower-level seats and 2,000 upper-level seats. What is the ratio of lower-level seats to total seats?
   - (A) $\frac{4}{9}$
   - (B) $\frac{4}{13}$
   - (C) $\frac{9}{13}$
   - (D) $\frac{9}{4}$

3. In a class of 20 students, how many conversations must be had so that every student talks to every other student in the class?
   - (A) 40
   - (B) 190
   - (C) 380
   - (D) 760

4. Convert 8 pounds, 8 ounces to kilograms to the nearest tenth of a kilogram.
   - (A) 3.9 kilograms
   - (B) 4.1 kilograms
   - (C) 17.6 kilograms
   - (D) 18.7 kilograms

5. If an employee who makes $37,500 per year receives a 5.5% raise, what is the employee's new salary?
   - (A) $35,437.50
   - (B) $35,625.00
   - (C) $39,375.00
   - (D) $39,562.50

6. Miguel works at a car dealership and is paid a 2 percent commission on every car he sells. If he sells one car for $15,000 and two cars for $12,900 each, how much will he be paid in commissions?
   - (A) $300
   - (B) $558
   - (C) $816
   - (D) $5,580

7. A teacher has 50 notebooks to hand out to students. If she has 16 students in her class, and each student receives 2 notebooks, how many notebooks will she have left over?
   - (A) 2
   - (B) 16
   - (C) 18
   - (D) 32

8. 40% of what number is equal to 17?
   - (A) 2.35
   - (B) 6.8
   - (C) 42.5
   - (D) 235

9. During a baseball team's practice, players spent 1 hour at batting practice, 30 minutes catching fly balls, and 15 minutes running sprints. What percentage of the practice did the players spend running sprints?

(A) 14.3
(B) 16.7
(C) 28.6
(D) 33.3

10. Michael is making cupcakes. He plans to give $\frac{1}{2}$ of the cupcakes to a friend and $\frac{1}{3}$ of the cupcakes to his coworkers. If he makes 48 cupcakes, how many will he have left over?

(A) 8
(B) 10
(C) 12
(D) 16

11. If the smallest angle in a non-right triangle is 20° and the shortest side is 14, what is the length of the longest side if the largest angle is 100°?

(A) 12.78
(B) 34.31
(C) 40.31
(D) 70.02

12. Students board a bus at 7:45 a.m. and arrive at school at 8:20 a.m. How long are the students on the bus?

(A) 30 minutes
(B) 35 minutes
(C) 45 minutes
(D) 50 minutes

13. Cone A is similar to cone B with a scale factor of 3:4. If the volume of cone A is 54π, what is the volume of cone B?

(A) 72π
(B) 128π
(C) 162π
(D) 216π

14. An ice chest contains 24 sodas, some regular and some diet. The ratio of diet soda to regular soda is 1:3. How many regular sodas are there in the ice chest?

(A) 1
(B) 4
(C) 6
(D) 18

15. Three people have winning lottery tickets and will split the $500,000 prize between them in a ratio of 3:2:1. How much money will go to the person receiving the most money?

(A) $83,333
(B) $166,666
(C) $250,000
(D) $333,333

16. Kim and Chris are writing a book together. Kim wrote twice as many pages as Chris, and together they wrote 240 pages. How many pages did Chris write?

(A) 80
(B) 100
(C) 120
(D) 160

17. If there are 10 millimeters in 1 centimeter, how many millimeters are in 150 centimeters?

(A) 1.5 mm
(B) 15 mm
(C) 150 mm
(D) 1500 mm

PRACTICE TEST TWO 73

18. Noah and Jennifer have a total of $10.00 to spend on lunch. If each buys his or her own order of french fries and a soda, how many orders of chicken strips can they share?

Menu

ITEM	PRICE
Hamburger	$4.00
Chicken Strips	$4.00
Onion Rings	$3.00
French Fries	$2.00
Soda	$1.00
Shake	$1.00

(A) 0
(B) 1
(C) 2
(D) 3

19. A store owner purchased 30 refrigerators at a price of $850. He sold them at a 15 percent markup over the price he paid. If he sold all 30 refrigerators, what was his total profit?

(A) $127.50
(B) $977.50
(C) $3,425
(D) $3,825

20. Out of 1,560 students at Ward Middle School, 15% want to take French. Which expression represents how many students want to take French?

(A) 1560 ÷ 15
(B) 1560 × 15
(C) 1560 × 0.15
(D) 1560 ÷ 0.15

21. The number of chairs in the front row of a movie theater is 14. Each subsequent row contains 2 more seats than the row in front of it. If the theater has 25 rows, what is the total number of seats in the theater?

(A) 336
(B) 350
(C) 888
(D) 950

22. The mean of 13 numbers is 30. The mean of 8 of these numbers is 42. What is the mean of the other 5 numbers?

(A) 5.5
(B) 10.8
(C) 16.4
(D) 21.2

23. If a student answers 42 out of 48 questions correctly on a quiz, what percentage of questions did she answer correctly?

(A) 82.5%
(B) 85%
(C) 86%
(D) 87.5%

24. Robbie has a bag of treats that contains 5 pieces of gum, 7 pieces of taffy, and 8 pieces of chocolate. If Robbie reaches into the bag and randomly pulls out a treat, what is the probability that Robbie will get a piece of taffy?

(A) $\frac{1}{13}$
(B) $\frac{1}{7}$
(C) $\frac{7}{20}$
(D) $\frac{7}{13}$

25. A map is drawn with a scale of 1 inch = 25 miles. If two cities are 115 miles apart, how far apart will they be on the map?

(A) 2.6 inches
(B) 2.9 inches
(C) 3.2 inches
(D) 4.6 inches

26. What is the percent increase in an employee's salary if it is raised from $57,000 to $60,000?

(A) 0.3%
(B) 0.4%
(C) 4%
(D) 5%

27. Kendrick has $2,386.52 in his checking account. If he pays $792.00 for rent, $84.63 for groceries, and $112.15 for his car insurance, how much money will he have left in his account?

(A) $1,397.74
(B) $1,482.37
(C) $1,509.89
(D) $2,189.22

28. If a car uses 8 gallons of gas to travel 650 miles, how many miles can it travel using 12 gallons of gas?

(A) 870 miles
(B) 895 miles
(C) 915 miles
(D) 975 miles

29. A person earning a salary between $75,000 and $100,000 per year will pay $10,620 in taxes plus 20% of any amount over $75,000. What would a person earning $80,000 per year pay in taxes?

(A) $10,620
(B) $11,620
(C) $12,120
(D) $12,744

30. A group of 20 friends is planning a road trip. They have 3 cars that seat 4 people, 3 cars that seat 5 people, and 1 car that seats 6 people. What is the fewest number of cars they can take on the trip if each person needs his or her own seat?

(A) 3 cars
(B) 4 cars
(C) 5 cars
(D) 6 cars

Word Knowledge

This part of the test measures your knowledge of words and their meanings. For each question, you are to choose the word below that is closest in meaning to the underlined word above.

1. Solicitous most nearly means
   (A) attentive.
   (B) persuasive.
   (C) cheerful.
   (D) serene.

2. Aptitude most nearly means
   (A) talent for socializing.
   (B) constant hunger.
   (C) capacity to learn.
   (D) love of pleasure.

3. The enemy would not capitulate, so the battle continued for days.
   (A) shrink
   (B) benefit
   (C) surrender
   (D) appear

4. Jeopardy most nearly means
   (A) prediction.
   (B) danger.
   (C) choice.
   (D) destiny.

5. Substantial most nearly means
   (A) partial.
   (B) inferior.
   (C) plentiful.
   (D) upright.

6. Acrimonious most nearly means
   (A) bitter.
   (B) inedible.
   (C) smoky.
   (D) rotten.

7. "Can't you people be quiet and let me sleep?" cried Pablo in a querulous tone.
   (A) furious
   (B) weary
   (C) frantic
   (D) complaining

8. Inclement most nearly means
   (A) hostile.
   (B) sparse.
   (C) stormy.
   (D) distressing.

9. Conciliatory most nearly means
   (A) wise.
   (B) tender.
   (C) moderate.
   (D) peacemaking.

10. The employee made an egregious error, and his employer fired him immediately.
    (A) flagrant
    (B) accidental
    (C) minor
    (D) agreeable

11. Taciturn most nearly means
    (A) aloof.
    (B) penniless.
    (C) agreeable.
    (D) changeable.

12. Concurrent most nearly means
    (A) up to date.
    (B) surging.
    (C) splashy.
    (D) simultaneous.

13. Elusive most nearly means
    (A) mysterious.
    (B) underhanded.
    (C) slimy.
    (D) snakelike.

14. When the wedding was canceled at the last moment, everyone's festive mood instantly deflated.
    (A) blew up
    (B) collapsed
    (C) changed
    (D) lifted

15. Complicity most nearly means
    (A) self-satisfaction.
    (B) creation—often of an artwork.
    (C) participation—often in a crime.
    (D) straightforwardness.

16. Relegate most nearly means
    (A) assign.
    (B) demote.
    (C) survey.
    (D) distribute.

17. After a fitful sleep, he woke up feeling exhausted.
    (A) deep
    (B) calming
    (C) suitable
    (D) disturbed

18. Monolithic most nearly means
    (A) single-minded.
    (B) intimidating.
    (C) colossal.
    (D) stony.

19. To lampoon most nearly means to
    (A) pierce.
    (B) capture.
    (C) ridicule.
    (D) cheer.

20. Patriarch most nearly means
    (A) patriotic person.
    (B) gentle leader.
    (C) huge doorway.
    (D) head man.

21. It seems gratuitous to punish someone with both humiliation and a hefty fine—one or the other would suffice.
    (A) raspy
    (B) appreciative
    (C) spontaneous
    (D) unreasonable

22. Sensory most nearly means
    (A) weather-related.
    (B) regretful.
    (C) critical.
    (D) physical.

23. Qualitative most nearly means
    (A) licensed.
    (B) unfamiliar.
    (C) based on size, number, or amount.
    (D) based on good and bad characteristics.

24. After we raze the dilapidated garage, our backyard will be almost twice as large as before.
    (A) repair
    (B) demolish
    (C) remodel
    (D) neglect

25. Obsequious most nearly means
    (A) apparent.
    (B) ignorant.
    (C) submissive.
    (D) repressive.

26. Misanthropic most nearly means
    (A) having a fear of spiders.
    (B) calm and philosophical.
    (C) having a fear of flying.
    (D) distrustful and reclusive.

27. Scientific research requires meticulous data collection and experimentation.
    (A) precise
    (B) supersized
    (C) welcoming
    (D) slow-moving

28. Noxious most nearly means
    (A) unfriendly.
    (B) poisonous.
    (C) irritating.
    (D) smooth.

29. Felicity most nearly means
    (A) catlike.
    (B) emotion.
    (C) irrelevance.
    (D) contentment.

30. Chivalrous most nearly means
    (A) warlike.
    (B) courteous.
    (C) hounded.
    (D) cowardly.

31. To expropriate something most nearly means to
    (A) steal it.
    (B) leave it.
    (C) collect it.
    (D) buy it.

32. To ebb most nearly means to
    (A) drift.
    (B) network.
    (C) motivate.
    (D) recede.

33. It is inappropriate to act like a buffoon during an important business meeting.
    (A) child
    (B) monkey
    (C) clown
    (D) spoilsport

34. Iconoclast most nearly means
    (A) symbol.
    (B) rebel.
    (C) fastener.
    (D) inference.

35. Mr. Axlerod is an opportunist, and he never passes up a chance to make a killing on the stock market.
    (A) a lucky person
    (B) an employer
    (C) a speculator
    (D) a lazy person

PARAGRAPH COMPREHENSION

This part of the test measures your ability to read and understand written material. Each passage is followed by a multiple-choice question. You are to choose the option that best answers the question based on the passage. No additional information or specific knowledge is needed.

Between November 15 and December 21, 1864, Major General William Tecumseh Sherman marched Union troops from the recently captured city of Atlanta to the port of Savannah. The goal was not only to capture the port city and secure Georgia for the Union, but also to destroy the Confederacy's infrastructure and demoralize its people. Sherman and his troops destroyed rail lines and burned buildings and fields. They packed only twenty days' worth of rations, foraging for the rest of their supplies from farms along the way. By the time they reached Savannah, they had destroyed 300 miles of railroad, countless cotton gins and mills, seized 4,000 mules, 13,000 head of cattle, 9.5 million pounds of corn, and 10.5 million pounds of fodder. Sherman estimated his troops inflicted $100 million in damages.

1. It can be inferred from the passage that the Confederacy
   (A) strongly resisted the actions of Sherman's troops.
   (B) was greatly weakened by the destruction.
   (C) used Sherman's March as a rallying point.
   (D) was relatively unaffected by the march.

In an effort to increase women's presence in government, several countries in Latin America, including Argentina, Brazil, and Mexico, have implemented legislated candidate quotas. These quotas require that at least 30 percent of a party's candidate list in any election cycle consists of women who have a legitimate chance at election. As a result, Latin America has the greatest number of female heads of government in the world, and the second highest percentage of female members of parliament after Nordic Europe. However, these trends do not carry over outside of politics. While 25 percent of legislators in Latin America are now women, less than 2 percent of CEOs in the region are female.

2. What is the main idea of the passage?
   (A) In Latin America, political parties must nominate women for office.
   (B) Latin America is the region with the greatest gender equality.
   (C) Women in Latin America have greater economic influence than political influence.
   (D) Women have a significant presence in Latin American politics.

At midnight on Saturday, August 12, 1961, units of the East German army moved into position and began closing the border between East and West Berlin. Destroying streets that ran parallel to the border to make them impassable, they installed ninety-seven miles of barbed wire and fences around West Berlin and another twenty-seven miles along the border between West and East Berlin. By Sunday morning the border was completely shut down. Families woke up that morning suddenly divided, and some East Berliners with jobs in the west were unable to get to work. West Berlin was now an isolated island surrounded by a communist government hostile to its existence.

3. The primary purpose of the passage is to
  (A) describe the impact of the closing of the Berlin border.
  (B) analyze East Germany's motives for closing the Berlin border.
  (C) explain the Western response to the closing of the Berlin border.
  (D) inform the reader about the methods used to close the Berlin border.

In a remote nature preserve in northeastern Siberia, scientists are attempting to recreate the subarctic steppe grassland ecosystem that flourished there during the last Ice Age. The area today is dominated by forests, but the lead scientists of the project believe the forested terrain was neither a natural development nor environmentally advantageous. They believe that if they can restore the grassland, they will be able to slow climate change by slowing the thawing of the permafrost which lies beneath the tundra. Key to this undertaking is restoring the wildlife to the region, including wild horses, musk oxen, bison, and yak. Most ambitiously, the scientists hope to revive the wooly mammoth species which was key in trampling the ground and knocking down the trees, helping to keep the land free for grasses to grow.

4. In the fourth sentence, the word *advantageous* most nearly means
  (A) beneficial
  (B) damaging
  (C) useful
  (D) appropriate

The Scream of Nature by Edvard Munch is one of the world's best known and most desirable artworks. While most people think of it as a single painting, the iconic creation actually has four different versions: two paintings and two pastels. In 2012, one of the pastels earned the fourth highest price paid for a painting at auction when it was sold for almost $120 million. The three others are not for sale; the Munch Museum in Oslo holds a painted version and a pastel version, while the National Gallery in Oslo holds the other painting. However, the desire to acquire them has been just as strong: in 1994 the National Gallery's version was stolen, and in 2004 the painting at the Munch Museum was stolen at gunpoint in the middle of the day. Both paintings were eventually recovered.

5. The primary purpose of the passage is to
  (A) describe the image depicted in *The Scream in Nature*.
  (B) explain the origin of the painting *The Scream in Nature*.
  (C) clarify the number of versions of *The Scream in Nature* that exist.
  (D) prove the high value of *The Scream in Nature*.

It could be said that the great battle between the North and South we call the Civil War was a battle for individual identity. The states of the South had their own culture, one based on farming, independence, and the rights of both man and state to determine their own paths. Similarly, the North had forged its own identity as a center of centralized commerce and manufacturing. This clash of lifestyles was bound to create tension, and this tension was bound to lead to war. But people who try to sell you this narrative are wrong. The Civil War was not a battle of cultural identities—it was a battle about slavery. All other explanations for the war are either a direct consequence of the South's desire for wealth at the expense of her fellow man or a fanciful invention to cover up this sad portion of our nation's history. And it cannot be denied that this time in our past was very sad indeed.

6. What is the main idea of the passage?
- **(A)** The Civil War was the result of cultural differences between the North and South.
- **(B)** The Civil War was caused by the South's reliance on slave labor.
- **(C)** The North's use of commerce and manufacturing allowed it to win the war.
- **(D)** The South's belief in the rights of man and state cost the war.

The cisco, a foot-long freshwater fish native to the Great Lakes, once thrived throughout the basin but had virtually disappeared by the 1950s. However, today fishermen are pulling them up by the net-load in Lake Michigan and Lake Ontario. It is highly unusual for a native species to revive, and the reason for the cisco's reemergence is even more unlikely. The cisco have an invasive species, quagga mussels, to thank for their return. Quagga mussels depleted nutrients in the lakes, harming other species highly dependent on these nutrients. Cisco, however, thrive in low-nutrient environments. As other species—many invasive—diminished, cisco flourished in their place.

7. It can be inferred from the passage that most invasive species
- **(A)** support the growth of native species.
- **(B)** do not impact the development of native species.
- **(C)** struggle to survive in their new environments.
- **(D)** cause the decline of native species.

Increasingly, companies are turning to subcontracting services rather than hiring full-time employees. This provides companies with many advantages like greater flexibility, reduced legal responsibility to employees, and lower possibility of unionization within the company. However, it has also led to increasing confusion and uncertainty over the legal definition of employment. Recently, the courts have grappled with questions about the hiring company's responsibility in maintaining fair labor practices. Companies argue that they delegate that authority to the subcontractors, while unions and other worker advocate groups argue that companies still have a legal obligation to the workers who contribute to their business.

8. The primary purpose of the passage is to
- **(A)** critique the labor practices of modern companies.
- **(B)** explain why companies prefer subcontracting work.
- **(C)** highlight a debate within the business and labor community.
- **(D)** describe a recent court decision related to labor practices.

For thirteen years, a spacecraft called *Cassini* has been on an exploratory mission to Saturn. The spacecraft was designed not to return but to end its journey by diving into Saturn's atmosphere. This dramatic ending will provide scientists with unprecedented information about Saturn's atmosphere and its magnetic and gravitational fields. First, however, *Cassini* will pass Saturn's largest moon, Titan, where it will record any changes in Titan's curious methane lakes, gathering information about potential seasons on the planet-sized moon. Then it will pass through the unexplored region between Saturn itself and its famous rings. Scientists hope to learn how old the rings are and to directly examine the particles that make them up. It is likely that the spectacular end to *Cassini* will introduce new questions for future exploration.

9. According to the passage, scientists want to learn more about Titan's
    (A) gravity, based on examination of its magnetic field.
    (B) rings, based on the particles that compose them.
    (C) seasons, based on changes to its lakes.
    (D) age, based on analysis of its minerals and gases.

Archaeologists have discovered the oldest known specimens of bedbugs in a cave in Oregon where humans once lived. The three different species date back to between 5,000 and 11,000 years ago. The finding gives scientists a clue as to how bedbugs became human parasites. These bedbugs, like those that plague humans today, originated as bat parasites. Scientists hypothesize that it was the co-habitation of humans and bats in the caves that encouraged the bugs to begin feeding on the humans. The three species found in the Oregon caves are actually still around today, although they continue to prefer bats. Humans only lived seasonally in the Oregon cave system, however, which might explain why these insects did not fully transfer to human hosts like bedbugs elsewhere did.

10. With which of the following claims about bedbugs would the author most likely agree?
    (A) Modern bedbugs that prefer humans thrive better in areas with extensive light.
    (B) Bedbugs are a relatively fragile species that has struggled to survive over time.
    (C) The transition to humans significantly accelerated the growth of bedbug populations.
    (D) Bedbugs that prefer humans originated in caves that humans occupied year-round.

Alexander Hamilton and James Madison called for the Constitutional Convention to write a constitution as the foundation of a stronger federal government. Madison and other Federalists like John Adams believed in separation of powers, republicanism, and a strong federal government. Despite the separation of powers that would be provided for in the US Constitution, anti-Federalists like Thomas Jefferson called for even more limitations on the power of the federal government.

11. In the context of the passage below, which of the following would most likely NOT support a strong federal government?
    (A) Alexander Hamilton
    (B) James Madison
    (C) John Adams
    (D) Thomas Jefferson

One of the most dramatic acts of nonviolent resistance in India's movement for independence from Britain came in 1930, when independence leader Mahatma Gandhi organized a 240-mile march to the Arabian Sea. The goal of the march was to make salt from seawater, in defiance of British law. The British prohibited Indians from collecting or selling salt—a vital part of the Indian diet—requiring them instead to buy it from British merchants and pay a heavy salt tax. The crowd of marchers grew along the way to tens of thousands of people. In Dandi, Gandhi picked up a small chunk of salt and broke British law. Thousands in Dandi followed his lead as did millions of fellow protestors in coastal towns throughout India. In an attempt to quell the civil disobedience, authorities arrested more than 60,000 people across the country, including Gandhi himself.

12. With which of the following claims about civil disobedience would the author most likely agree?

- **(A)** Civil disobedience is a disorganized form of protest easily quashed by government.
- **(B)** Civil disobedience requires extreme violations of existing law to be effective.
- **(C)** Civil disobedience is an effective strategy for effecting political change.
- **(D)** Civil disobedience is only effective in countries that already have democracy.

Alfie closed his eyes and took several deep breaths. He was trying to ignore the sounds of the crowd, but even he had to admit that it was hard not to notice the tension in the stadium. He could feel 50,000 sets of eyes burning through his skin—this crowd expected perfection from him. He took another breath and opened his eyes, setting his sights on the soccer ball resting peacefully in the grass. One shot, just one last shot, between his team and the championship. He didn't look up at the goalie, who was jumping nervously on the goal line just a few yards away. Afterward, he would swear he didn't remember anything between the referee's whistle and the thunderous roar of the crowd.

13. Which of the following conclusions is best supported by the passage?

- **(A)** Alfie passed out on the field and was unable to take the shot.
- **(B)** The goalie blocked Alfie's shot.
- **(C)** Alfie scored the goal and won his team the championship.
- **(D)** The referee declared the game a tie.

The Gatling gun, a forerunner of the modern machine gun, was an early rapid-fire spring loaded, hand-cranked weapon. In 1861, Dr. Richard J. Gatling designed the gun to allow one person to fire many shots quickly. His goal was to reduce the death toll of war by decreasing the number of soldiers needed to fight. The gun consisted of a central shaft surrounded by six rotating barrels. A soldier turned a crank which rotated the shaft. As each barrel reached a particular point in the cycle, it fired, ejected its spent cartridge and loaded another. During this process, it cooled down, preparing it to fire again. The Gatling gun was first used in combat by the Union Army during the Civil War. However, each gun was purchased directly by individual commanders. The US Army did not purchase a Gatling gun until 1866.

14. The primary purpose of the passage is to

- **(A)** explain why the Gatling gun was harmful to troops.
- **(B)** critique the US Army's use of the Gatling gun.
- **(C)** describe the design and early history of the Gatling gun.
- **(D)** analyze the success of Dr. Gatling in achieving his goals.

After looking at five houses, Robert and I have decided to buy the one on Forest Road. The first two homes we visited didn't have the space we need—the first had only one bathroom, and the second did not have a guest bedroom. The third house, on Pine Street, had enough space inside but didn't have a big enough yard for our three dogs. The fourth house we looked at, on Rice Avenue, was stunning but well above our price range. The last home, on Forest Road, wasn't in the neighborhood we wanted to live in. However, it had the right amount of space for the right price.

15. What is the author's conclusion about the house on Pine Street?

   (A) The house did not have enough bedrooms.
   (B) The house did not have a big enough yard.
   (C) The house was not in the right neighborhood.
   (D) The house was too expensive.

Math Knowledge

This part of the test measures your knowledge of mathematical terms and principles. Each problem is followed by four possible answers. You are to decide which one of the four choices is correct.

1. A cube is inscribed in a sphere such that each vertex on the cube touches the sphere. If the volume of the sphere is 972π cm³, what is the approximate volume of the cube in cubic centimeters?

    (A) 9
    (B) 104
    (C) 927
    (D) 1125

2. $\frac{7}{8} - \frac{1}{10} - \frac{2}{3} =$

    (A) $\frac{1}{30}$
    (B) $\frac{4}{120}$
    (C) $\frac{13}{120}$
    (D) $\frac{4}{21}$

3. If $j = 4$, what is the value of $2(j-4)^4 - j + \frac{1}{2}j$?

    (A) 0
    (B) −2
    (C) 2
    (D) 4

4. Solve for y: $3y + 2x = 15z$

    (A) $y = \frac{3}{15z} - 2x$
    (B) $y = \frac{-2x + 15z}{3}$
    (C) $y = -\frac{2}{3}x + 15z$
    (D) $y = -2x + 5z$

5. Which of the following is equivalent to $54z^4 + 18z^3 + 3z + 3$?

    (A) $18z^4 + 6z^3 + z + 1$
    (B) $3z(18z^3 + 6z^2 + 1)$
    (C) $3(18z^4 + 6z^3 + z + 1)$
    (D) $72z^7 + 3z$

6. What is the area of the shape?

    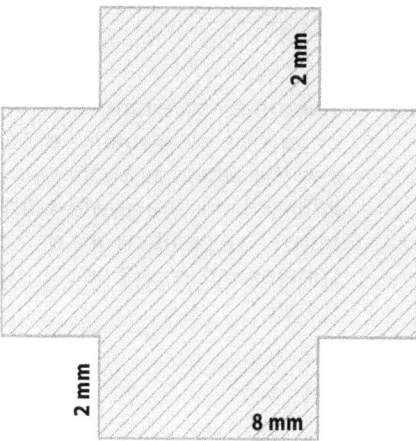

    (A) 6 mm²
    (B) 16 mm²
    (C) 64 mm²
    (D) 128 mm²

7. 50 shares of a financial stock and 10 shares of an auto stock are valued at $1,300. If 10 shares of the financial stock and 10 shares of the auto stock are valued at $500, what is the value of 50 shares of the auto stock?

    (A) $30
    (B) $20
    (C) $1,300
    (D) $1,500

8. Solve for x: $4x + 12 = x - 3$

    (A) $x = -5$
    (B) $x = -3$
    (C) $x = 1.8$
    (D) $x = 5$

9. Simplify: $\left(\dfrac{4x^{-3}y^4z}{8x^{-5}y^3z^{-2}}\right)^2$

(A) $\dfrac{x^4yz^3}{2}$

(B) $\dfrac{x^4y^2z^6}{2}$

(C) $\dfrac{x^4y^2z^6}{4}$

(D) $\dfrac{x^4yz^3}{4}$

10. Two spheres are tangent to each other. One has a volume of 36π, and the other has a volume of 288π. What is the greatest distance between a point on one of the spheres and a point on the other sphere?

(A) 6
(B) 9
(C) 18
(D) 36

11. Factor $4a^3b + 10ab^2$

(A) $ab(4a^2 + 5b^2)$
(B) $ab(a^2b + 10b)$
(C) $2ab(2a^2 + 5b)$
(D) $2a^2b(2ab + 5)$

12. What is 498,235 rounded to the nearest thousands?

(A) 498,000
(B) 498,200
(C) 499,000
(D) 499,200

13. Which of the following is the y-intercept of the given equation?

$7y - 42x + 7 = 0$

(A) $(0, \frac{1}{6})$
(B) $(6, 0)$
(C) $(0, -1)$
(D) $(-1, 0)$

14. The value $(3 + \sqrt{2})(3 - \sqrt{2})$ is equal to

(A) 7
(B) 9
(C) 13
(D) $9 - 2\sqrt{2}$

15. A wedge from a cylindrical piece of cheese was cut as shown. If the entire wheel of cheese weighed 73 pounds before the wedge was removed, what is the approximate remaining weight of the cheese?

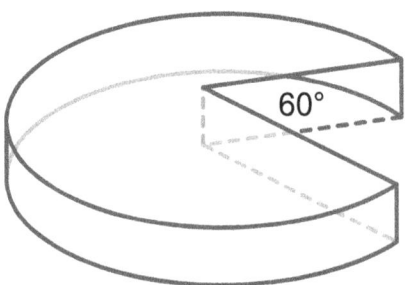

(A) 12.17 pounds
(B) 37.00 pounds
(C) 55.00 pounds
(D) 60.83 pounds

16. Which of the following is a solution to the inequality $2x + y \leq -10$?

(A) $(0, 0)$
(B) $(10, 2)$
(C) $(10, 10)$
(D) $(-10, -10)$

17. Solve for x.

$x = 6(3^0)$

(A) 0
(B) 1
(C) 6
(D) 18

18. The sum of the internal angles of a quadrilateral is
    (A) 90°
    (B) 180°
    (C) 270°
    (D) 360°

19. $(3x + 2)^2 =$
    (A) $9x^2 + 4$
    (B) $9x^2 + 36$
    (C) $9x^2 + 6x + 4$
    (D) $9x^2 + 12x + 4$

20. If the volume of a cube is 343 cubic meters, what is the cube's surface area?
    (A) 49 m^2
    (B) 84 m^2
    (C) 196 m^2
    (D) 294 m^2

21. What is the distance on the x,y-coordinate plane between the points (3, 0) and (−2, −5)?
    (A) $\sqrt{6}$
    (B) $\sqrt{10}$
    (C) $\sqrt{29}$
    (D) $5\sqrt{2}$

22. What is the value of $3x + 7y - 4$ if $x = 8$ and $y = 2$?
    (A) 34
    (B) 38
    (C) 42
    (D) 58

23. If one leg of a right triangle has a length of 40, which of the following could be the lengths of the two remaining sides?
    (A) 50 and 41
    (B) 9 and 41
    (C) 9 and 30
    (D) 50 and 63

24. The formula for distance is $d = v \times t$, where v is the object's velocity and t is the time. How long will it take a plane to fly 4,000 miles from Chicago to London if the plane flies at a constant rate of 500 mph?
    (A) 0.125 hours
    (B) 3.5 hours
    (C) 8 hours
    (D) 20 hours

25. Multiply the terms $3x^2yz^4$ and $6xy^3z^2$.
    (A) $9x^2y^3z^8$
    (B) $9x^3y^4z^6$
    (C) $18xy^2z^2$
    (D) $18x^3y^4z^6$

Electronics

This part of the test measures your knowledge of electronics. Each of the questions or incomplete statements is followed by four choices. You are to decide which one of the choices best answers the question or completes the statement.

1. Two negative charges are held at a distance of 1 m from each other. When the charges are released, they will
   - (A) remain at rest.
   - (B) move closer together.
   - (C) move farther apart.
   - (D) move together in the same direction.

2. Current is measured in
   - (A) ohms.
   - (B) amperes.
   - (C) volts.
   - (D) coulombs.

3. What is the electrical difference between a conducting material and an insulating material?
   - (A) There is no electrical difference.
   - (B) A conducting material will conduct electricity, and an insulating material will not.
   - (C) A conducting material creates electrons, and an insulating material destroys them.
   - (D) An insulating material will create heat when electricity flows through it, and a conducting material will not.

4. What part of an electrical circuit is at zero potential and can accept any amount of current?
   - (A) fuse
   - (B) power supply
   - (C) ground
   - (D) circuit breaker

5. Why do electronics become hot?
   - (A) Current is the same as heat, so all electronics are hot.
   - (B) The resistivity, or resistance, of the materials creates heat when current flows through them.
   - (C) When electrons hit the walls of the wires and other circuit elements, they create heat.
   - (D) Electronics are designed to become hot because current will only flow in hot materials.

6. What is the voltage across a 1 kΩ resistor if 1 mA is flowing through it?
   - (A) 0.1 V
   - (B) 1 V
   - (C) 10 V
   - (D) 100 V

7. A voltage supply is connected to a load. The measured voltage across the supply is 121 V, and the current measured through the load is 850 mA. What is the power used by the load?
   - (A) 0.1 W
   - (B) 102.9 W
   - (C) 142.4 W
   - (D) 102.9 kW

8. Which of the following devices stores charge?
   - (A) transistor
   - (B) capacitor
   - (C) diode
   - (D) rectifier

9. What is the equivalent resistance for the circuit below?

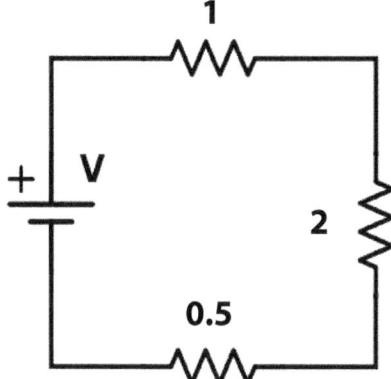

(A) 0.5 kΩ
(B) 1 kΩ
(C) 2 kΩ
(D) 3.5 kΩ

10. What is wire gauge?
(A) It is related to the length of the wire.
(B) It is related to the cross-sectional area of the wire and is measured with a gauge.
(C) It is related to the material composition of the wire.
(D) It is related to the strength of the cladding (outer plastic cover) of the wire.

11. Which case would NOT result in a short circuit?
(A) a tree branch falling on power lines
(B) water or drink spilled onto a computer while it is on
(C) placing a wire across the terminals of a battery
(D) water or drink spilled onto a computer while it is off

12. When dopants are added to a semiconductor to make it P-type, what is the dominant charge carrier in the material?
(A) neutrons
(B) protons
(C) negative charges from electrons
(D) positive charges from holes

13. What is the current running through a 15 Ω resistor when a voltage of 45 V is applied across it?
(A) 3 A
(B) 30 A
(C) 67.5 A
(D) 675 A

14. What is the direction of the magnetic field?
(A) always from a north pole to a south pole
(B) always from a south pole to a north pole
(C) always from an east pole to a west pole
(D) always from a west pole to an east pole

15. A person moves from the US to Europe and finds that her electronics, built for US electrical power at 120 V, will not work with European power at 240 V. She buys a transformer that converts 120 V to 240 V. If the primary (input) coil in this transformer has 1,000 turns, how many turns does the secondary (output) coil have?
(A) 500 turns
(B) 1,000 turns
(C) 2,000 turns
(D) 4,000 turns

16. What is the name of a generator that produces a DC supply?

(A) alternator
(B) rectifier
(C) dynamo
(D) invertor

17. What is the benefit of a compound motor?

(A) It is cheaper to build.
(B) It has very little torque and is very slow.
(C) It has a large starting torque and is good at maintaining rotation speed.
(D) It has a very high rotation speed.

18. The symbol below is used to represent which part of a circuit?

(A) voltmeter
(B) cell
(C) capacitor
(D) resistor

19. A circuit with one 10 Ω resistor has a current of 25 A. How much voltage is being applied to the circuit.

(A) 2.5 V
(B) 4 V
(C) 40 V
(D) 250 V

20. In a solid-state device, electricity flows through a

(A) insulator.
(B) vacuum.
(C) semiconductor.
(D) transistor.

Automotive and Shop Information

This part of the test measures your knowledge of automotive and shop information. Each of the questions or incomplete statements is followed by four choices. You are to decide which one of the choices best answers the question or completes the statement.

1. What does a pick-up coil monitor?
   (A) plug wire spark
   (B) battery
   (C) reluctor
   (D) coil voltage

2. Which gripping tool can cut and squeeze?
   (A) needle-nose pliers
   (B) adjustable joint pliers
   (C) lineman pliers
   (D) locking pliers

3. What part cleans up the waste exhaust from the engine?
   (A) header pipe
   (B) exhaust recirculation valve
   (C) muffler
   (D) catalytic converter

4. Which operation is a micrometer used for?
   (A) measuring the outside diameter of a shaft
   (B) measuring the inside diameter of a bore
   (C) measuring the length of boards
   (D) measuring the tension of a spring

5. After disassembling an engine block, an inspection of the cooling jacket freeze plug area reveals burred areas inside the hole. Which file is used to remove burrs?
   (A) triangular file
   (B) flat file
   (C) rasp
   (D) Robertson screwdriver

6. What is the unibody?
   (A) a plastic shell
   (B) a solid floor piece
   (C) a one-piece complete body
   (D) stressed skin design

7. What tool is used to cut a circular hole in a board?
   (A) circular saw
   (B) snap-ring pliers
   (C) miter saw
   (D) hole saw

8. What kind of joint connects to the transaxle?
   (A) CV
   (B) universal
   (C) ball
   (D) ball or universal, depending on the make

9. Which tool is designed to remove roll pins from a bore?
   (A) Vernier caliper
   (B) roll-pin punch
   (C) center punch
   (D) drift punch

10. What is negative camber?
    (A) inward tilt of the wheel
    (B) outward tilt of the wheel
    (C) forward tilt of the wheel
    (D) rearward tilt of the wheel

11. What tool is used to remove screws with a square hole in the head?
    (A) Torx screwdriver
    (B) Phillips screwdriver
    (C) Robertson screwdriver
    (D) ratchet

12. What is the purpose of bleeding brake lines?
    (A) to remove excess fluid
    (B) to remove dirt
    (C) to allow the brakes to be applied to the rear rotor or drum
    (D) to remove air

13. What tool is used to measure the threads of a bolt?
    (A) tap
    (B) Vernier caliper
    (C) inside caliper
    (D) thread-pitch gauge

14. What does a bridge rectifier do in the electrical system?
    (A) It charges the battery.
    (B) It converts AC to DC.
    (C) It supplies power to the alternator.
    (D) It converts DC to AC.

15. Which wrench has a jaw that moves with a thumbwheel?
    (A) box-end wrench
    (B) combination wrench
    (C) adjustable wrench
    (D) open-end wrench

16. What does a knock sensor detect?
    (A) when the vehicle is in a crash
    (B) when the piston knocks against the cylinder wall
    (C) detonation
    (D) raw exhaust

17. A fleet vehicle has a flat tire. Which tool(s) is/are used to remove lug nuts quickly?
    (A) ratchet and socket
    (B) impact wrench and impact socket
    (C) combination wrench
    (D) box-end wrench

18. What does the tire pressure monitoring system activate?
    (A) traction control
    (B) electronic stability control
    (C) LATCH system
    (D) a light on the dash

19. What tool is designed to install a framing nail?
    (A) claw hammer
    (B) rubber mallet
    (C) chuck and key
    (D) hand drill

20. What is required for ignition in a diesel engine?
    (A) a fuel injector
    (B) a spark plug located in the pre-chamber
    (C) a spark plug in the cylinder head
    (D) an indirect injected process

21. A fleet vehicle cylinder head bolt has to be removed. The bolt is in an open area, and there are many cylinder head bolts to be removed. Which tool combination is used to remove the bolts quickly?
    (A) ratchet and socket
    (B) combination wrench
    (C) open-end wrench
    (D) box-end wrench

22. Manufacturers are required by law to emit less than a certain amount of
   - **(A)** hydrocarbons, carbon monoxide, and nitrogen dioxide.
   - **(B)** hydrocarbons, carbon dioxide, and nitrogen dioxide.
   - **(C)** hydrocarbons, oxygen, and carbon dioxide.
   - **(D)** water, carbon dioxide, and oxygen.

23. Which tool is a keyless chuck commonly used with?
   - **(A)** hand drill
   - **(B)** band saw
   - **(C)** nail gun
   - **(D)** drill press

24. Cold air is
   - **(A)** good for the air intake.
   - **(B)** bad for the air intake.
   - **(C)** heavier than hot air.
   - **(D)** lighter than hot air.

25. Which hammer is commonly used in metalworking operations?
   - **(A)** claw hammer
   - **(B)** rubber mallet
   - **(C)** wooden mallet
   - **(D)** ball-peen hammer

Mechanical Comprehension

This part of the test measures your knowledge of mechanics. Each of the questions or incomplete statements is followed by four choices. You are to decide which one of the choices best answers the question or completes the statement.

1. A 1,000 kg mass is accelerating at 10 m/s². What is the net force causing this acceleration?
   (A) 0 N
   (B) 1,000 N
   (C) 10,000 N
   (D) 100,000 N

2. What type of lever is shown below?

   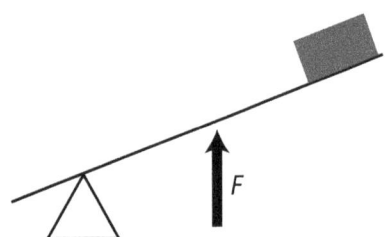

   (A) first-class
   (B) second-class
   (C) third-class
   (D) fourth-class

3. Which statement is not an accurate description of force?
   (A) Force is equal to an object's mass times its acceleration.
   (B) Every action will have an equal and opposite reaction.
   (C) The net force will always be zero.
   (D) A mass will remain at constant velocity unless a force is applied.

4. A machine performs 100 J of work in 10 s. What is the power used by the machine?
   (A) 0 W
   (B) 10 W
   (C) 100 W
   (D) 1,000 W

5. What is the mechanical advantage for a machine that produces an output force of 4,000 N from an input force of 1,000 N?
   (A) 0
   (B) 4
   (C) 1,000
   (D) 4,000

6. A constant force of 10 N is applied to a mass of 10 kg, which leads to an acceleration of 1 m/s². If the mass of the object is doubled, what will be the object's new acceleration?
   (A) 0 m/s²
   (B) 0.5 m/s²
   (C) 1 m/s²
   (D) 10 m/s²

7. Which of the following is not a fundamental force?
   (A) gravitation
   (B) nuclear
   (C) electromagnetic
   (D) friction

8. Which of the following terms defines friction?
   (A) a force that opposes motion
   (B) a force that pushes down onto a surface
   (C) a force that rotates an object
   (D) a force that increases the force of gravity

9. Find the net force on a mass experiencing an applied force of 100 N and a friction force of 90 N as shown below.

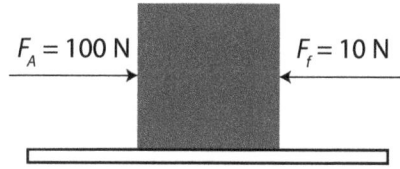

(A) 10 N
(B) 90 N
(C) 100 N
(D) 190 N

10. What is the mechanical advantage of a wheel and axis if the axle radius (input) is 0.1 m and the wheel radius (output) is 0.5 m?

(A) $\frac{1}{10}$
(B) $\frac{1}{5}$
(C) $\frac{1}{4}$
(D) $\frac{1}{3}$

11. For a mass resting on an inclined plane, the normal force

(A) will be less than if the mass were on a horizontal plane.
(B) will be more than if the mass were on a horizontal plane.
(C) is always the same.
(D) only exists when a mass is on a horizontal plane.

12. A box with a volume of 1 m³ is fully submerged in a liquid with a density of 100 kg/m³. What is the mass of the liquid displaced by the box?

(A) 1 kg
(B) 10 kg
(C) 100 kg
(D) 1,000 kg

13. What is the kinetic energy of a mass of 10 kg that is moving at 2 m/s?

(A) 10 J
(B) 20 J
(C) 30 J
(D) 40 J

14. A ball is dropped from rest and falls due to gravity at 9.8 m/s² toward the center of the earth. What is its speed after 1 second?

(A) 0 m/s
(B) 4.9 m/s
(C) 9.8 m/s
(D) 14.7 m/s

15. What is the most common source of thermal energy (heat) from mechanical motion?

(A) friction
(B) potential energy
(C) work
(D) gravity

16. Which of the following materials is best used to decrease the force of an impact?

(A) wood chips
(B) glass
(C) porcelain tile
(D) steel

17. The total momentum of a system before a collision is 200 kg m/s. What is the total momentum of the system after the collision?

(A) 0 kg m/s
(B) 100 kg m/s
(C) 200 kg m/s
(D) 400 kg m/s

18. A person has a weight of 300 N and is standing on the floor. What is the magnitude and direction of the normal force from the floor?

(A) 300 N up toward the person
(B) 300 N down toward the floor
(C) 150 N up toward the person
(D) 150 N down toward the floor

19. What is the mechanical advantage of the screw shown below?

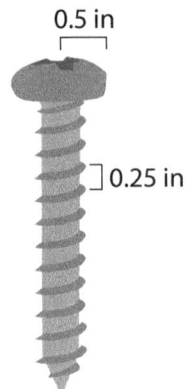

(A) 1π
(B) 2π
(C) 3π
(D) 4π

20. The magnetic force and electric force on a charge each have a magnitude of 10 N and point in the same direction. For a mass of 10 kg, what is the acceleration of the charge?

(A) 0 m/s²
(B) 1 m/s²
(C) 2 m/s²
(D) 3 m/s²

21. How far will a car moving at 40 m/s travel in 2 s?

(A) 10 m
(B) 20 m
(C) 40 m
(D) 80 m

22. A man is pushing against a heavy rock sitting on a flat plane, and the rock is not moving. The force that holds the rock in place is

(A) friction.
(B) gravity.
(C) normal force.
(D) buoyant force.

23. A box sliding down a ramp is being acted on by all of the following forces except

(A) tension.
(B) gravity.
(C) friction.
(D) normal force.

24. What is the gear ratio for an input gear with 1,000 teeth and an output gear with 3,500 teeth?

(A) 3.5
(B) 35
(C) 350
(D) 3,500

25. What is the torque experienced by a wrench that is turned using 4 N of force at a distance of 0.5 m from the axis of rotation?

(A) 2 Nm
(B) 8 Nm
(C) 20 Nm
(D) 80 Nm

Assembling Objects

Given a set of objects, your task is to determine which answer choice shows how the objects will look once the parts are put together.

1.

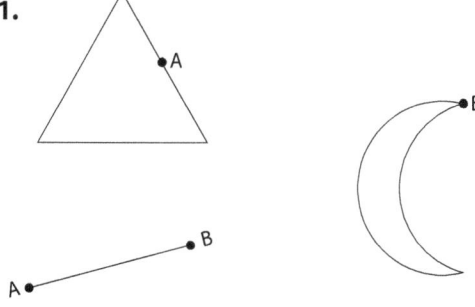

(A)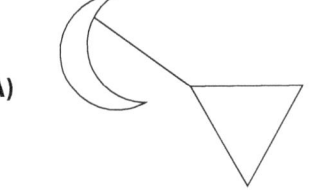

(B)

(C)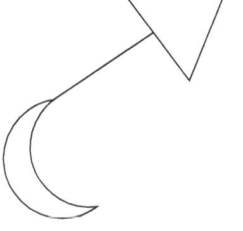

(D)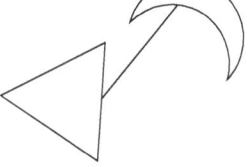

2.

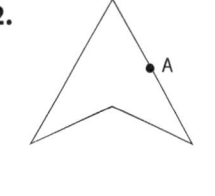

 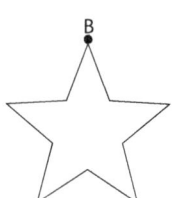

(A)

(B)

(C)

(D)

3.

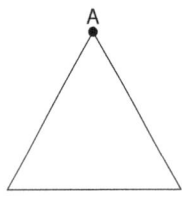
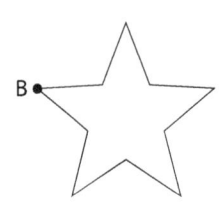

(A)

(C)

(B)

(D)

4.

(A)

(C)

(B)

(D)

5.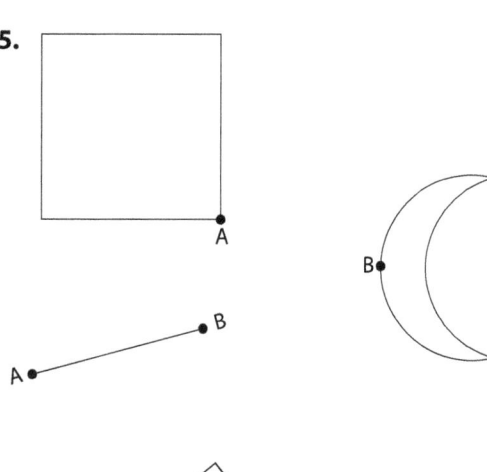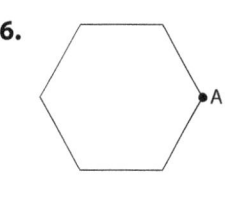

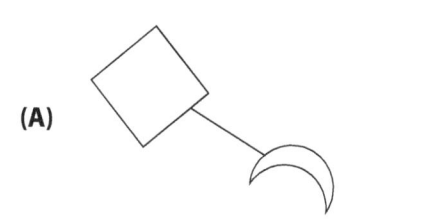 

(A)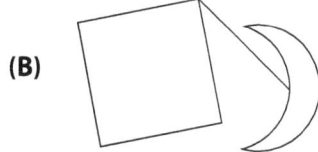

(B)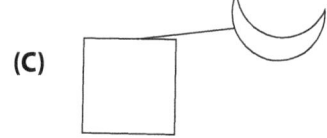

(C)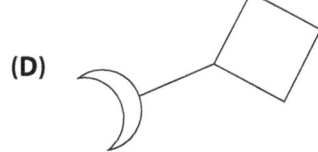

(D)

6.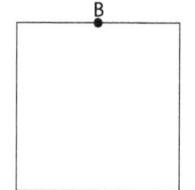

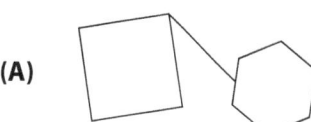

(A)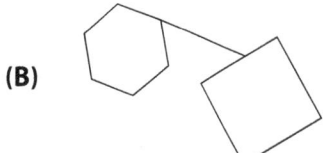

(B)

(C)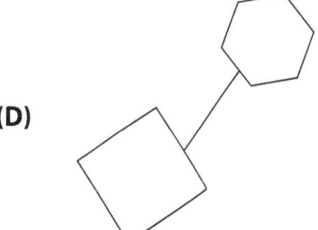

(D)

PRACTICE TEST TWO 99

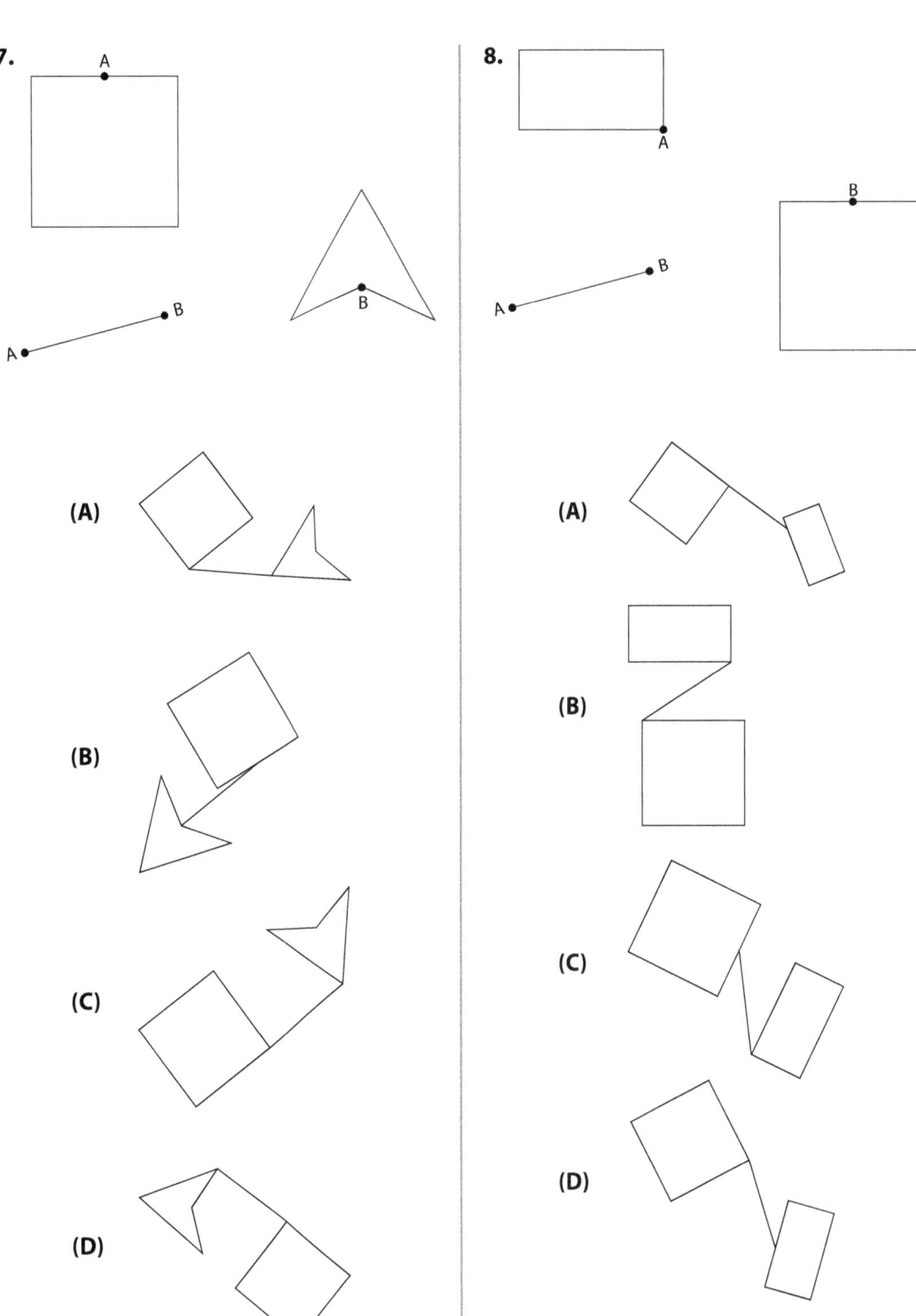

9.

10.

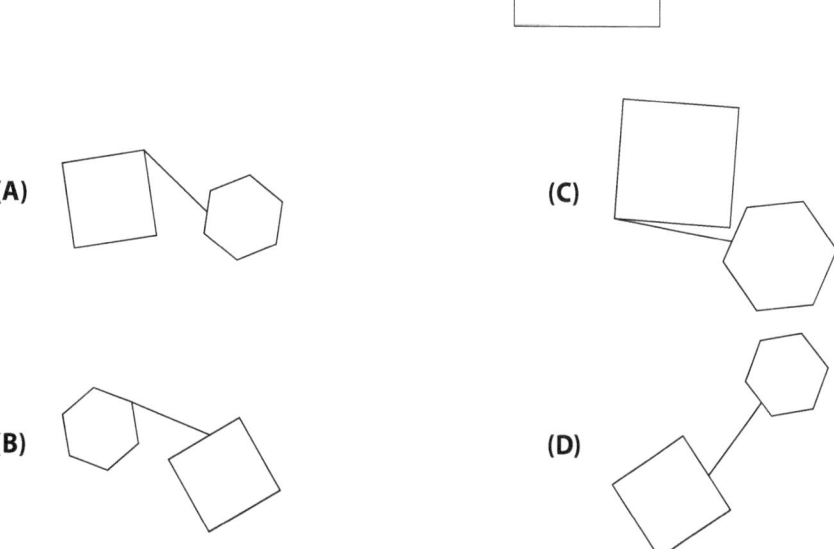

PRACTICE TEST TWO 101

11.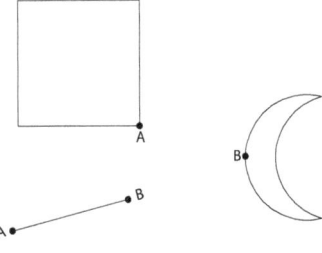

(A)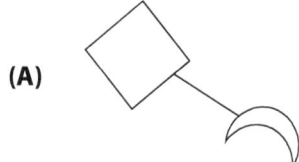

(B)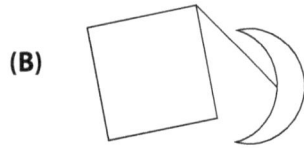

(C)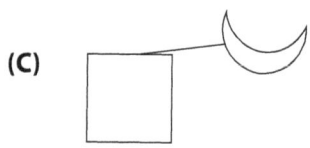

(D)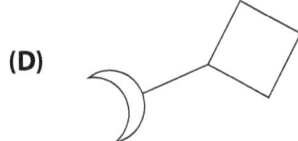

12.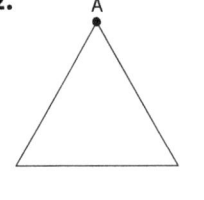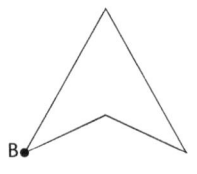

(A)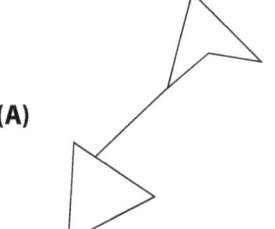

(B)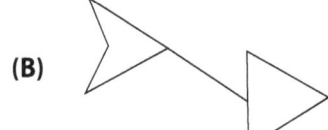

(C)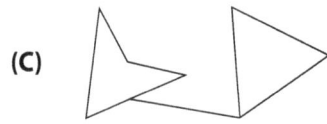

(D)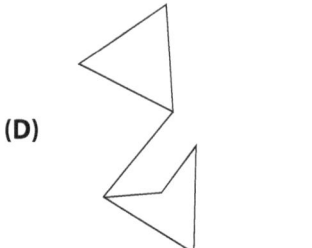

13.

(A) (C)

(B) (D)

14.

(A) (C)

(B) (D)

15.

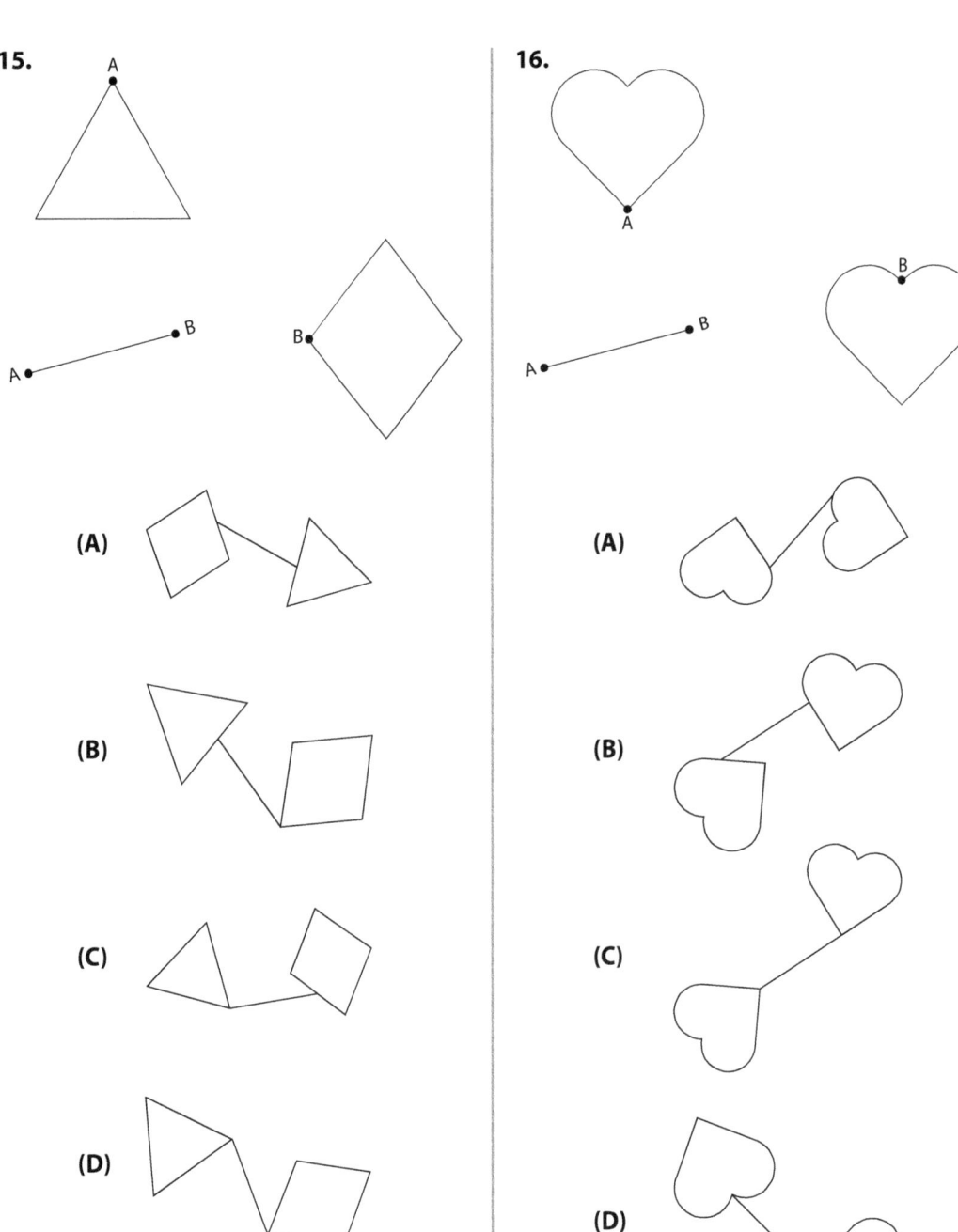

16.

17.

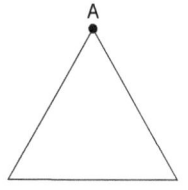

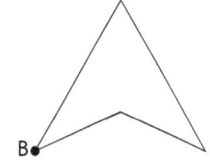

(A)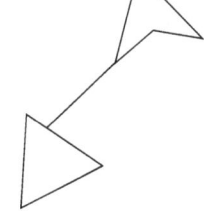

(C)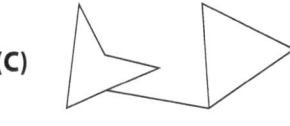

(B)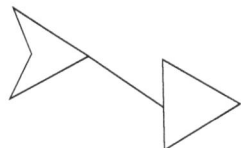

(D)

18.

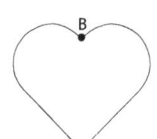

(A)

(C)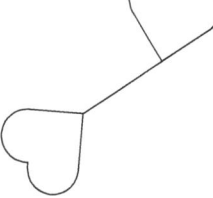

(B)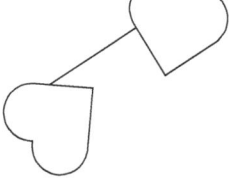

(D)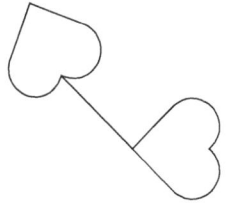

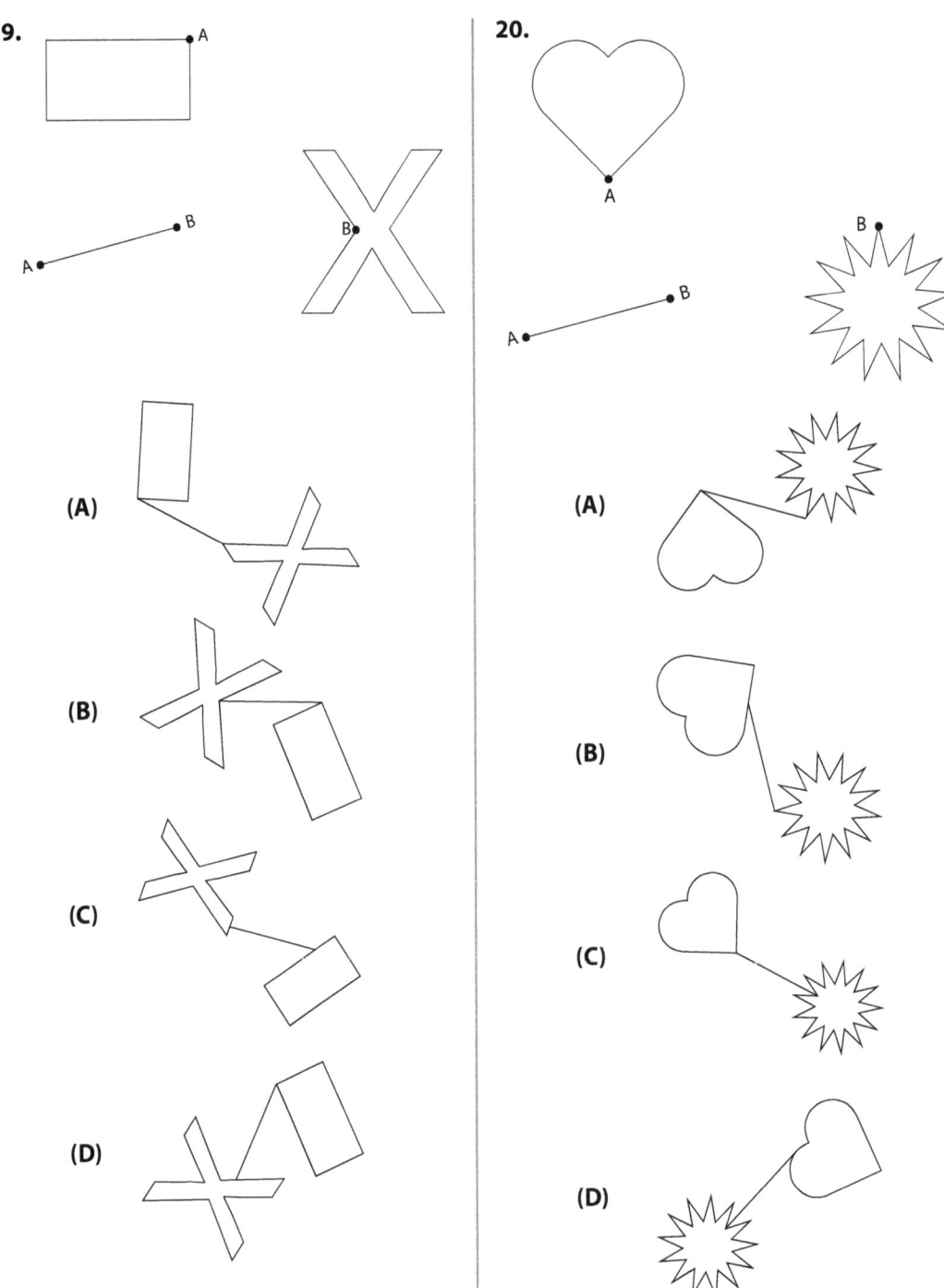

21.

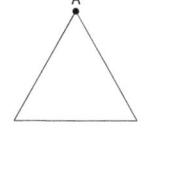  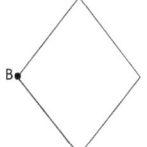

(A)    (C)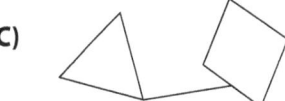

(B)    (D)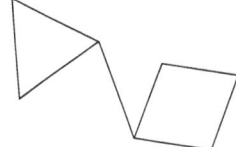

22.

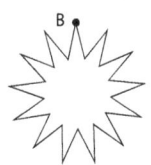

(A)    (C)

(B)    (D)

PRACTICE TEST TWO 107

23.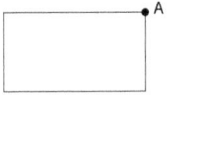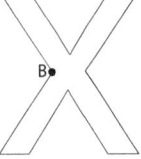

(A)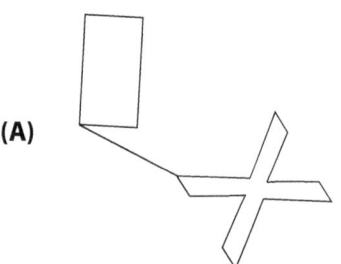

(B)

(C)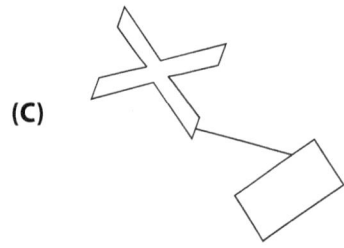

(D)

24.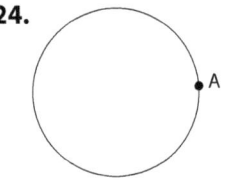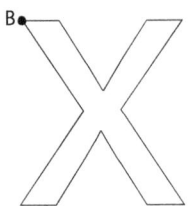

(A)

(B)

(C)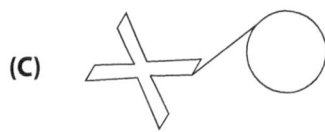

(D)

25.

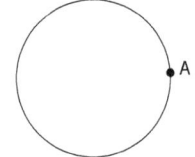
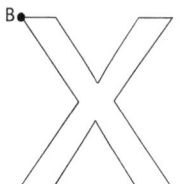

(A)

(C)

(B)

(D)

ANSWER KEY

GENERAL SCIENCE

1. **(A)**

   (A) is correct. The kidneys filter waste from the blood.

   (B) is incorrect. The hypothalamus produces hormones that control the pituitary gland.

   (C) is incorrect. The testes produce hormones that control male sexual characteristics.

   (D) is incorrect. The thyroid produces hormones that control growth and metabolism.

2. **(D)**

   (A) is incorrect. Mitochondria release chemical energy from glucose to be used by the cell.

   (B) is incorrect. Cytoplasm provides support to the cell.

   (C) is incorrect. Vacuoles store water.

   (D) is correct. Ribosomes are responsible for production of proteins.

3. **(A)**

   (A) is correct. The sun is about ninety-three million miles from Earth; the next closest star is about twenty-five trillion miles away.

   (B) is incorrect. The moon orbits Earth.

   (C) is incorrect. Earth is always closer to the sun than Jupiter is.

   (D) is incorrect. Mercury is the closest planet to the sun, but Venus is closer to Earth.

4. **(B)**

   (A) is incorrect. In mutualism, both organisms benefit.

   (B) is correct. Parasitism describes a relationship in which one organism benefits from another organism, to the detriment of the host organism.

   (C) is incorrect. Commensalism is when one organism benefits from another without causing harm to the host organism.

   (D) is incorrect. Predation is individual organisms consuming others for food; it is not a long-term relationship.

5. **(D)**

   (A) is incorrect. Roots extract water and minerals from the soil.

   (B) is incorrect. The stem transports nutrients to other parts of the plant.

   (C) is incorrect. The bark is dead tissue on the surface of the stem.

(D) is correct. Through photosynthesis, leaves use the sun's energy to convert carbon dioxide into glucose.

6. **(A)**

    (A) is correct. Geysers are caused by geothermal heating of water underground.

    (B) is incorrect. Glaciers are formed when snow and ice do not melt before new layers of snow and ice are added.

    (C) is incorrect. Tsunamis are caused by earthquakes on the ocean floor.

    (D) is incorrect. Tornadoes are caused by instability of warm, humid air in the lower atmosphere mixing with cool air in the upper atmosphere.

7. **(C)**

    (A) is incorrect. Mass is the amount of matter in an object. Weight is a measure of the gravitational pull on an object. Weight changes in space, but mass does not.

    (B) is incorrect. Weight is created by gravitational pull, not mass.

    (C) is correct. Weight is a force created by gravitational pull.

    (D) is incorrect. The surface area or size of an object does not indicate the mass of that object.

8. **(A)**

    (A) is correct. Alveoli are the tiny sacs in the lungs that are the site of gas exchange.

    (B) is incorrect. The bronchi are the passages through which air spreads into the lungs.

    (C) is incorrect. The lungs are divided into lobes.

    (D) is incorrect. The trachea move air into the bronchi.

9. **(B)**

    (A) is incorrect. A solar eclipse is when the moon moves between the sun and Earth.

    (B) is correct. A lunar eclipse is when Earth moves between the moon and the sun.

    (C) is incorrect. A black hole is a collapsed star with tremendous gravitational pull.

    (D) is incorrect. A supernova is an explosion of the core of a star.

10. **(D)**

    (A) is incorrect. An enzyme is not a lipid, which are fats.

    (B) is incorrect. DNA is a type of nucleic acid.

    (C) is incorrect. RNA is a type of nucleic acid.

    (D) is correct. An enzyme is a protein that catalyzes a reaction.

11. **(D)**

    (A) is incorrect. Helium is found in large quantities on the sun. It is an inert, colorless, tasteless gas.

    (B) is incorrect. Oxygen makes up about 20 percent of Earth's atmosphere.

    (C) is incorrect. Seventy-eight percent of Earth's atmosphere is made of nitrogen, and nitrogen is essential for all living organisms.

    (D) is correct. Carbon dioxide is formed when fossil fuels containing carbon are burned. Excess carbon dioxide is responsible for global warming.

12. **(A)**

    (A) is correct. A warm front is when a warm air mass moves into a cold air mass.

    (B) is incorrect. A cold front is when a cold air mass moves into a warm air mass.

    (C) is incorrect. An isobar is a contour line indicating locations of equal barometric pressures.

    (D) is incorrect. A tornado is caused by unstable air.

13. **(C)**

    (A) is incorrect. Invasive species are species that arrive in a community from a different location and drive down the population of native species.

(B) is incorrect. Climate changes, such as the Ice Age and global warming, are responsible for the extinction of a species.

(C) is correct. Habitat conservation restores the natural habitat of organisms, protecting a species.

(D) is incorrect. Overexploitation by humans through hunting for sport, animal testing, and illegal trapping has caused the endangerment of many species.

14. **(A)**

   (A) is correct. Neurons typically have one long, thick axon that transmits signals away from the neuron.

   (B) is incorrect. The dendrite is the part of the neuron that receives information.

   (C) is incorrect. A stimulus is an event which triggers a response from a neuron.

   (D) is incorrect. The myelin sheath insulates the axon and increases its efficiency.

15. **(D)**

   (A) is incorrect. Plastic is an insulator. Insulators block the flow of heat from one object to another.

   (B) is incorrect. Rubber is an insulator.

   (C) is incorrect. Porcelain is an insulator.

   (D) is correct. Aluminum is a good thermal conductor because heat energy can move easily through it.

16. **(D)**

   (A) is incorrect. A tracheotomy is not a body system reaction; it is a medical intervention.

   (B) is incorrect. Max's muscles, tendons, and ligaments are part of the muscular system. The bending of joints is a normal function, not a way to maintain homeostasis.

   (C) is incorrect. Excessive production of growth hormones is an example of disease.

   (D) is correct. Homeostasis refers to body systems working together to ensure that factors such as temperature and oxygen levels are optimal. Shivering is a mechanism for creating needed warmth.

17. **(D)**

   (A) is incorrect. Wavelength is the distance between cycles of a wave. It does not affect how large an object appears to be.

   (B) is incorrect. Diffraction occurs when waves pass through a narrow opening and then spread out.

   (C) is incorrect. Amplitude is the height of a wave; it affects how loud a sound is perceived to be.

   (D) is correct. Lenses refract, or bend, light waves to make objects appear larger.

18. **(A)**

   (A) is correct. Only the first two planets, Mercury and Venus, lack moons.

   (B) is incorrect. Earth has one moon.

   (C) is incorrect. Jupiter has many moons.

   (D) is incorrect. Saturn has many moons.

19. **(A)**

   (A) is correct. Reptiles like crocodiles have scaly skin, are hatched from eggs on land, and are cold-blooded.

   (B) is incorrect. Amphibians like frogs are hatched from eggs in water, have gills but develop lungs, and become land animals as they mature.

   (C) is incorrect. Salamanders are amphibians.

   (D) is incorrect. Fish like salmon live in water; they also have a backbone, gills, scales, and fins.

20. **(D)**

   (A) is incorrect. Adenine is a nucleotide found in DNA.

(B) is incorrect. Guanine is a nucleotide found in DNA.

(C) is incorrect. Thymine is a nucleotide found in DNA.

(D) is correct. Uracil (U) is a pyrimidine found in RNA, replacing the thymine (T) pyrimidine found in DNA.

21. **(A)**

    (A) is correct. A heterogeneous mixture is any nonuniform mixture, and the parts of soil are distributed unevenly.

    (B) is incorrect. Salt water is a homogenous mixture in which the salt in uniformly distributed.

    (C) is incorrect. Steel is a homogenous mixture of iron and other elements, usually carbon.

    (D) is incorrect. Air is a homogenous mixture of many different molecules, including oxygen and nitrogen gases and water vapor.

22. **(B)**

    (A) is incorrect. The amplitude is the distance from the wave's midline to its crest or trough.

    (B) is correct. Wavelength is the length of each cycle of the wave, which can be found by measuring between crests.

    (C) is incorrect. Frequency is the number of cycles a wave passes through during a time period.

    (D) is incorrect. Period is the time it takes for a wave to complete one cycle.

23. **(D)**

    (A) is incorrect. All mixtures, whether saturated or unsaturated, have a solute and solvent that are not chemically bonded.

    (B) is incorrect. The state of the solute and solvent has no effect on whether the solution is saturated.

    (C) is incorrect. A solution with an evenly distributed solute is homogenous, and it may be saturated or unsaturated.

    (D) is correct. No more solute can be dissolved into a saturated solution.

24. **(D)**

    (A) is incorrect. Fungi cannot perform photosynthesis, and so cannot produce their own energy.

    (B) is incorrect. Fungi are not consumers.

    (C) is incorrect. Fungi are not consumers.

    (D) is correct. Most fungi derive their energy by breaking down dead plant and animal matter.

25. **(C)**

    (A) is incorrect. Mitosis does not quarter the number of chromosomes in the daughter cells.

    (B) is incorrect. Meiosis produces daughter cells with half the number of chromosomes in the parent cell.

    (C) is correct. Mitosis creates daughter cells with the same number of chromosomes as the parent cell.

    (D) is incorrect. Mitosis does not double the number of chromosomes in the daughter cells.

ARITHMETIC REASONING

1. (D)

Use the formula for percentages.
part = whole × percent = 540 × 0.85
= **459**

2. (C)

total seats = 4,500 + 2,000
$\frac{\text{lower seats}}{\text{all seats}} = \frac{4,500}{6,500} = \frac{9}{13}$

3. (B)

Use the combination formula to find the number of ways to choose 2 people out of a group of 20.
$C(20, 2) = \frac{20!}{2!\,18!} = \mathbf{190}$

4. (A)

Multiply by the converstion factor to get from pounds to kilograms.
8 pounds, 8 ounces = 8.5 pounds
$8.5 \text{ lb.} \left(\frac{1 \text{ kg}}{2.2 \text{ lb.}}\right) = \mathbf{3.9 \text{ kg}}$

5. (D)

Find the amount of change and add to the original amount.
amount of change = original amount × percent change
= 37,500 × 0.055 = 2,062.50
37,500 + 2,062.50 = **$39,562.50**

6. (C)

Add the value of the three cars.
15,000 + 2(12,900) = 40,800
Use the formula for percentages to find the total commission.
part = whole × percent
= 40,800 × 0.02 = **$816**

7. (C)

If each student receives 2 notebooks, the teacher will need 16 × 2 = 32 notebooks. After handing out the notebooks, she will have 50 − 32 = **18 notebooks left**.

8. (C)

Use the equation for percentages.
$\text{whole} = \frac{\text{part}}{\text{percent}} = \frac{17}{0.4} = \mathbf{42.5}$

9. (A)

Convert each value into minutes, and use the formula for percentages to find the time spent running sprints.
$\text{percent} = \frac{\text{part}}{\text{whole}}$
$= \frac{15}{60 + 30 + 15} = 0.143 = \mathbf{14.3\%}$

10. (A)

Add the number of cupcakes he will give to his friend and to his coworkers, then subtract that value from 48.
# of cupcakes for his friend:
$\frac{1}{2} \times 48 = 24$
# of cupcakes for his coworkers:
$\frac{1}{3} \times 48 = 16$
48 − (24 + 16) = **8**

11. (C)

Use the law of sines.
$\frac{\sin 20°}{14} = \frac{\sin 100°}{x}$
$x = \frac{14(\sin 100°)}{\sin 20°}$
x = 40.31

12. (B)

There are 15 minutes between 7:45 a.m. and 8:00 a.m. and 20 minutes between 8:00 a.m. and 8:20 a.m.
15 minutes + 20 minutes = **35 minutes**

13. (B)

Set up a proportion. Cube the scale factor when calculating volume.
$\frac{54\pi}{x} = \frac{3^3}{4^3}$
x = 128π

14. (D)

One way to find the answer is to draw a picture.

PRACTICE TEST TWO ANSWER KEY 115

Put 24 cans into groups of 4. One out of every 4 cans is diet (light gray) so there is 1 light gray can for every 3 dark gray cans. That leaves 18 dark gray cans (regular soda).

Alternatively, solve the problem using ratios.

$\frac{Regular}{Total} = \frac{3}{4} = \frac{x}{24}$

$4x = 72$

$x = \mathbf{18}$

15. **(C)**

Set up a proportion and solve. Add the parts of the ratio together to find the whole.

$\frac{1}{3+2+1} = \frac{3}{6} = \frac{x}{500,000}$

$3(500,000) = 6x$

$x = \mathbf{\$250,000}$

16. **(A)**

p = number of pages written by Chris
$2p$ = number of pages written by Kim
$p + 2p = 240$
$p = \mathbf{80}$

17. **(D)**

$\frac{150 \text{ cm}}{1} \times \frac{10 \text{ mm}}{1 \text{ cm}} = \mathbf{1,500 \text{ mm}}$

18. **(B)**

Set up an equation to find the number of orders of chicken strips they can afford:

$\$10 - 2(\$2.00 + \$1.00) = x$
$\$10 - 2(\$3.00) = x$
$\$10 - \$6.00 = \$4.00$

Four dollars is enough money to buy 1 order of chicken strips to share.

19. **(D)**

Find the amount the store owner paid for the refrigerators.
$850 \times 30 = 25,500$
Find the amount the owner will earn for the refrigerators.
sale price = $850(1.15) = 977.50$
$977.50 \times 30 = 29,325$

Subtract the amount the owner paid from the amount he earned to find his profits.
$29,325 - 25,500 = \mathbf{\$3,825}$

20. **(C)**

Use the formula for finding percentages. Express the percentage as a decimal.
part = whole × percent = **1560 × 0.15**

21. **(D)**

Use the formula for an arithmetic sum.
$S_n = \frac{n}{2}(2a_1 + (n-1)d)$
$= \frac{25}{2}(2(14) + (25-1)2) = \mathbf{950}$

22. **(B)**

Find the sum of the 13 numbers whose mean is 30.
$13 \times 30 = 390$
Find the sum of the 8 numbers whose mean is 42.
$8 \times 42 = 336$
Find the sum and mean of the remaining 5 numbers.
$390 - 336 = 54$
$\frac{54}{5} = \mathbf{10.8}$

23. **(D)**

Use the formula for percentages.
$percent = \frac{part}{whole}$
$= \frac{42}{48}$
$= 0.875 = \mathbf{87.5\%}$

24. **(C)**

Use the equation for probability.
$probability = \frac{possible\ favorable\ outcomes}{all\ possible\ outcomes}$
$= \frac{7}{(5+7+8)}$
$= \mathbf{\frac{7}{20}}$

25. **(D)**

Set up a proportion and solve.
$\frac{1 \text{ in.}}{25 \text{ miles}} = \frac{x \text{ in.}}{115 \text{ miles}}$
$1(115) = 25x$
$x = \mathbf{4.6 \text{ inches}}$

26. (D)
Use the formula for percent increase.
$$precent\ increase = \frac{amount\ of\ change}{original\ amount}$$
$$= \frac{3,000}{60,000} = 0.05 = \mathbf{5\%}$$

27. (A)
Subtract the amount of the bills from the amount in the checking account.
792.00 + 84.63 + 112.15 = 988.78
2,386.52 − 988.78 = **$1,397.74**

28. (D)
Set up a proportion and solve.
$$\frac{8}{650} = \frac{12}{x}$$
12(650) = 8x
x = 975 miles

29. (B)
Add the base amount and the tax on the extra percentage of the person's income.
10,620 + 0.2(80,000 − 75,000)
= **$11,620**

30. (B)
Add together the seats in the cars until there are 20.
6 + 5 = 11
6 + 5 + 5 = 16
6 + 5 + 5 + 5 = 21
The fewest number of cars that will seat 20 people is **4 cars**.

Word Knowledge

1. **(A)**

   Solicitous means "full of concern." For example, good waiters and waitresses are solicitous; they care about keeping their customers happy.

2. **(C)**

   Aptitude means "natural ability or tendency." For example, someone with an aptitude for math can learn mathematical concepts quickly and easily.

3. **(C)**

   Capitulate means "to surrender or give up."

4. **(B)**

   The word root *jeu* or *jocus* means "play, game, or joke" and the word root *partir* means "to divide." A divided game is a game of chance that involves great risk, so to be in jeopardy means to be in danger (of losing).

5. **(C)**

   Substantial means "an ample or considerable amount." For example, wealthy people have a substantial amount of money.

6. **(A)**

   The word root *ācer* in *acrid*, *acrimony*, and *acrimonious* means "sharp and sour," and the suffix *–ous* means "possessing or full of." And so, an acrimonious relationship is full of bitterness.

7. **(D)**

   The word root *queri* means "to complain," and the suffix *–ous* means "full of." And so, most people complain, grumble, and express grievances in a querulous tone.

8. **(C)**

   Inclement weather is stormy, windy, blustery, or otherwise severe.

9. **(D)**

   The word root *concili* means "council," the suffix *–ate* means "perform the action of," and the suffix *–ory* means "characterized by." And so, a conciliatory person is one who councils others to make peace.

10. **(A)**

    Egregious means "obviously and extremely bad."

11. **(A)**

    Taciturn means "reluctant or unwilling to talk." For example, a taciturn person may appear shy or uninterested in socializing with others.

12. **(D)**

    The prefix *con–* means "with or together," the word root *concurrere* means "to run together," and the suffix *–ent* means "doing a certain action." And so, two or more concurrent events happen at the same time, or simultaneously.

13. **(A)**

    Elusive means "hard to understand or identify." For example, in a mystery story, the solution to the crime may be elusive, or difficult to discover.

14. **(B)**

    The prefix *de–* means "negate," and the word root *flāre* means "to blow." When a balloon deflates, the air goes out of it and it collapses, and when someone's joyful mood deflates, it collapses.

15. **(C)**

    The prefix *com–* means "in association with," the word root *plex* means "to fold together," and the suffix *–ity* means "the act or condition of." And so, complicity is the act of working with someone on something—and sometimes that something is a crime.

16. **(A)**

    Relegate means "to assign to a particular place or situation." For example, a student might be relegated to stay after class to help clean the classroom.

17. **(D)**

    Fitful means "erratic or irregular." Someone who sleeps fitfully or erratically cannot get sufficient rest.

18. **(C)**

    The prefix *mono–* means "one," the word root *lith* means "stone," and the suffix *–ic* means "having some of the characteristics of." A monolith is a huge statue made from one stone, so a monolithic object is huge or colossal, like a monolith is.

19. **(C)**

    Lampoon means "to ridicule through satire." For example, political cartoons lampoon public figures by exaggerating and poking fun at their flaws and misdeeds.

20. **(D)**

    The word root *pater* means "father," and the word root *arkhein* means "to rule," so a patriarch is a man who leads his family.

21. **(D)**

    A gratuitous action is unwarranted, excessive, or uncalled for.

22. **(D)**

    Sensory means "relating to the senses, including sight, sound, taste, smell, and touch." For example, someone experiencing sensory overload is receiving too much information through his senses.

23. **(D)**

    The word root *quāl* means "of what sort," and the suffix *–ive* means "indicating a certain character," so a qualitative report evaluates someone or something based on qualities or characteristics.

24. **(B)**

    Raze means "to destroy or demolish." It is often used in the phrase "raze to the ground."

25. **(C)**

    Obsequious means "to show flattering attention." For example, an obsequious employee always defers to his boss and will do anything he is asked.

26. **(D)**

    The prefix *mis–* means "negating," the word root *anthropos* means "man or people," and the suffix *–ic* means "having certain traits." And so, a *misanthrope* or misanthropic person is someone who distrusts and dislikes most other people.

27. **(A)**

    The word root *metus* means "fear," and the suffix *–ous* means "possessing or full of." Over time the word *meticulous* came to mean "anxiously fussy." And so, a meticulous process is one that requires attention to detail in order to complete.

28. **(B)**

    Noxious means "physically or morally harmful." For example, a noxious gas can be lethal to people and animals.

29. **(D)**

    The word root *fēlīx* means "happy," and the suffix *–ity* means "the act or condition of," so felicity is contentment, joy, or happiness.

30. **(B)**

    The word root *chevalier* means "noble, brave, faithful knight," and the suffix *-ous* means "possessing the traits of," so a chivalrous person is brave, considerate, kind, and polite, especially to those who need protection.

31. **(A)**

    The prefix *ex-* means "out of or from," the word root *proprius* means "someone's possession," and the suffix *-ate* means "perform the action of." And so, to expropriate an item means to take it from the person it belongs to or to steal it.

32. **(D)**

    Ebb means "to fall or recede." For example, when an ocean tide ebbs, it recedes from shore.

33. **(C)**

    Buffoonery is frivolous or playful behavior.

34. **(B)**

    The word root *icon* means "image," and the word root *klast* means "to break." An image breaker is someone who rebels against established religion or leadership.

35. **(C)**

    The word root *opportunitatem* means "fitness, convenience, or favorable time," and the suffix *-ist* means "someone who believes in or practices a certain activity." And so, an opportunist is someone who believes in taking advantage of an opportunity, whether or not it is right to do so.

Paragraph Comprehension

1. (B)

(A) is incorrect. The author does not provide enough detailed evidence to reasonably infer the Confederate reaction to the march.

(B) is correct. The author describes the level of destruction in detail, suggesting it had a significant negative impact on the Confederacy.

(C) is incorrect. Again, as in option A, the author does not describe any response to the march.

(D) is incorrect. The author writes, "Sherman estimated his troops inflicted $100 million in damages."

2. (D)

(A) is incorrect. While this fact is stated in the passage, it is not the main idea.

(B) is incorrect. The author writes, "However, these trends do not carry over outside of politics."

(C) is incorrect. The author explains that women have a large amount of political influence but less economic influence.

(D) is correct. The passage discusses the large number of women in political positions in Latin America.

3. (A)

(A) is correct. The passage describes how the closing of the border affected the geography of the city and the lives of Berliners.

(B) is incorrect. The author does not explain why the border was closed.

(C) is incorrect. The author does not describe the response to the border closing.

(D) is incorrect. The author explains that the East German army closed off West Berlin using barbed wire and fences, but this is not the primary purpose of the passage.

4. (A)

(A) is correct. The author goes on to explain that the development of forests was not good for the environment: scientists believe grasslands would slow climate change.

(B) is incorrect. The author says that the forests are harmful to climate.

(C) is incorrect. The author explains that forests are harmful to the environment in this situation, and that grasslands would combat climate change. The word *useful* is too weak in this context.

(D) is incorrect. The word *appropriate* does not make sense in this context.

5. (D)

(A) is incorrect. The passage does not describe the actual artwork at all.

(B) is incorrect. The author names the artist who made the painting but states nothing else about its origin.

(C) is incorrect. While the author does state that there are four versions of the artwork, this is not the primary purpose of the passage.

(D) is correct. The author writes, "*The Scream of Nature* by Edvard Munch is one of the world's best known and most desirable artworks."

6. (B)

(A) is incorrect. The author asserts that, despite the popular narrative, cultural differences were not the cause of the Civil War.

(B) is correct. The author writes, "The Civil War was not a battle of cultural identities—it was a battle about slavery. All other explanations for the war are either a direct consequence of the South's desire for wealth at the expense of her fellow man or a fanciful invention to cover up this sad portion of our nation's history."

(C) is incorrect. The author does not discuss the strengths of the North or provide any reason for why it won the war.

(D) is incorrect. Though the author mentions these cultural beliefs, she does not suggest that these were the reasons the South was defeated.

7. **(D)**

    (A) is incorrect. The author provides no evidence that invasive species typically help native species.

    (B) is incorrect. The author writes that the quagga mussels, an invasive species, harmed native species.

    (C) is incorrect. The author implies that quagga mussels are thriving.

    (D) is correct. The author writes that "the reason for the cisco's reemergence is even more unlikely. The cisco have an invasive species, quagga mussels, to thank for their return."

8. **(C)**

    (A) is incorrect. The author does not express an opinion on labor practices.

    (B) is incorrect. While the author does explain the advantages of subcontracting for companies, this is not the primary purpose of the passage.

    (C) is correct. The author presents the reasons for the debate and both sides of the argument.

    (D) is incorrect. The author states that there have been related court cases but does not detail them.

9. **(C)**

    (A) is incorrect. The author discusses plans to study magnetic and gravitational fields on Saturn, not Titan.

    (B) is incorrect. The author writes, "Then it will pass through the unexplored region between Saturn itself and its famous rings." The passage does not mention any rings on Titan.

    (C) is correct. The author writes, "… it will record any changes in Titan's curious methane lakes, providing information about potential seasons on the planet-sized moon."

    (D) is incorrect. The author refers to the rings of Saturn, not to Titan, when stating, "Scientists hope to learn how old the rings are."

10. **(D)**

    (A) is incorrect. The author does not address the impact of light on bedbugs.

    (B) is incorrect. The author explains that the three discovered species still exist today.

    (C) is incorrect. The author does not address the growth rate of bedbug populations.

    (D) is correct. The author writes, "Humans only lived seasonally in the Oregon cave system, however, which might explain why these insects did not fully transfer to human hosts like bedbugs elsewhere did."

11. **(D)**

    (A) is incorrect. The author states that "Alexander Hamilton…called for the Constitutional Convention to write a constitution as the foundation of a stronger federal government."

    (B) is incorrect. The author states that "James Madison called for the Constitutional Convention to write a constitution as the foundation of a stronger federal government."

    (C) is incorrect. The author states that "Federalists like John Adams believed in… a strong federal government."

    (D) is correct. In the passage, Thomas Jefferson is defined as an anti-Federalist, in contrast with Federalists who believed in a strong federal government.

12. **(C)**

    (A) is incorrect. The author writes that the protest spread in spite of government attempts to end it.

    (B) is incorrect. The author writes, "In Dandi, Gandhi picked up a small chunk of salt and broke British law."

Picking up a piece of salt is not itself an extreme act; Gandhi was able to make a big statement with a small action.

(C) is correct. The author describes a situation in which civil disobedience had an enormous impact.

(D) is incorrect. The action the author describes occurred in India when it was controlled by Britain, a colonial and nondemocratic power.

13. **(C)**

    (A) is incorrect. Tough Alfie does not remember what happened, the phrase "doesn't remember anything between the referee's whistle and the thunderous roar of the crowd" indicates that he was able to take the shot.

    (B) is incorrect. The crowd "expected perfection from him [Alfie,]" so the reader can imply that the "thunderous roar" was a result of a successful goal.

    (C) is correct. The crowd's support for Alfie and their collective roar after the shot implies that Alfie scored the goal and won the championship.

    (D) is incorrect. The crowd "expected perfection from him [Alfie]," so the reader can imply that the "thunderous roar" was a result of a successful goal and a winning performance.

14. **(C)**

    (A) is incorrect. The author does not address the impact of the gun on troops.

    (B) is incorrect. The author does not offer an opinion on the use of the Gatling gun.

    (C) is correct. The author explains why the gun was created, how it functions, and how it was initially used.

    (D) is incorrect. The author does not describe the impact of Gatling gun on combat fatalities.

15. **(B)**

    (A) is incorrect. The author indicates that the house on Pine Street "had enough space inside[.]"

    (B) is correct. The author says that the house on Pine Street "had enough space inside but didn't have a big enough yard for [their] three dogs."

    (C) is incorrect. The author does not mention the neighborhood of the Pine Street house.

    (D) is incorrect. The author does not mention the price of the Pine Street house.

MATH KNOWLEDGE

1. **(D)**
   Use the formula for the volume of a sphere to find its radius.
   $V = \frac{4}{3}\pi r^3$
   $972\pi = \frac{4}{3}\pi r^3$
   $r = 9$

   Use the super Pythagorean theorem to find the side of the cube.
   $d^2 = a^2 + b^2 + c^2$
   $18^2 = 3s^2$
   $s \approx 10.4$

   Use the length of the side to find the volume of the cube.
   $V = s^3$
   $V \approx (10.4)^3$
   $V \approx \mathbf{1{,}125}$

2. **(C)**
   Convert each fraction to the LCD and subtract the numerators.
   $\frac{7}{8} - \frac{1}{10} - \frac{2}{3}$
   $= \frac{7}{8}\left(\frac{15}{15}\right) - \frac{1}{10}\left(\frac{12}{12}\right) - \frac{2}{3}\left(\frac{40}{40}\right)$
   $= \frac{105}{120} - \frac{12}{120} - \frac{80}{120} = \mathbf{\frac{13}{120}}$

3. **(B)**
   Plug 4 in for j and simplify.
   $2(j-4)^4 - j + \frac{1}{2}j$
   $2(4-4)^4 - 4 + \frac{1}{2}(4) = \mathbf{-2}$

4. **(B)**
   Isolate the variable y on one side of the equation.
   $3y + 2x = 15z$
   $3y = -2x + 15z$
   $\mathbf{y = \frac{-2x + 15z}{3}}$

5. **(C)**
   Factor the expression using the greatest common factor of 3.
   $54z^4 + 18z^3 + 3z + 3 =$
   $\mathbf{3(18z^4 + 6z^3 + z + 1)}$

6. **(D)**
   Find the area of the square as if it did not have the corners cut out.
   $12 \text{ mm} \times 12 \text{ mm} = 144 \text{ mm}^2$
   Find the area of the four cut out corners.
   $2 \text{ mm} \times 2 \text{ mm} = 4 \text{ mm}^2$
   $4(4 \text{ mm}^2) = 16 \text{ mm}^2$
   Subtract the area of the cut out corners from the large square to find the area of the shape.
   $144 \text{ mm}^2 - 16 \text{ mm}^2 = \mathbf{128 \text{ mm}^2}$

7. **(D)**
   Set up a system of equations and solve using elimination.
   $f =$ the cost of a financial stock
   $a =$ the cost of an auto stock
   $50f + 10a = 1{,}300$
   $10f + 10a = 500$
   $50f + 10a = 1{,}300$
   $+ -50f - 50a = -2{,}500$
   $-40a = -1{,}200$
   $a = 30$
   $50(30) = \mathbf{\$1{,}500}$

8. **(A)**
   Isolate the variable x on one side.
   $4x + 12 = x - 3$
   $3x = -15$
   $\mathbf{x = -5}$

9. **(C)**
   Use the rules of exponents to simplify the expression.
   $\left(\frac{4x^{-3}y^4z}{8x^{-5}y^3z^{-2}}\right)^2 = \left(\frac{x^2yz^3}{2}\right)^2 = \mathbf{\frac{x^4y^2z^6}{4}}$

10. **(C)**
    The greatest distance will be between two points at opposite ends of each sphere's diameters. Find the diameter of each sphere and add them.
    $36\pi = \frac{4}{3}\pi r_1^3$
    $r_1 = 3$

124 Elissa Simon ■ ASVAB Practice Test Book

$d_1 = 2(3) = 6$
$288\pi = \frac{4}{3}\pi r_2^3$
$r_2 = 6$
$d_2 = 2(6) = 12$
$d_1 + d_2 = 6 + 12 = \mathbf{18}$

11. **(C)**

    Factor the greatest common factor $2ab$ out of both terms.
    $4a3b + 10ab^2 = \mathbf{2ab(2a^2 + 5b)}$

12. **(A)**

    The 8 is in the thousands place. Because the value to the right of the 8 is less than 5, the 8 remains the same and all values to its right become zero. The result is **498,000**.

13. **(C)**

    Plug 0 in for x and solve for y.
    $7y - 42x + 7 = 0$
    $7y - 42(0) + 7 = 0$
    $y = -1$
    The y-intercept is at **(0, −1)**.

14. **(A)**

    Use FOIL to distribute.
    $(3 + \sqrt{2})(3 - \sqrt{2}) =$
    $3(3) + 3(-\sqrt{2}) + \sqrt{2}(3) + \sqrt{2}(-\sqrt{2})$
    $= 9 - 3\sqrt{2} + 3\sqrt{2} - 2 = \mathbf{7}$

15. **(D)**

    Set up a proportion to find the weight of the removed wedge.
    $\frac{60°}{x \text{ lb.}} = \frac{360°}{73 \text{ lb.}}$
    $x \approx 12.17$ lb.
    Subtract the removed wedge from the whole to find the weight of the remaining piece.
    $73 - 12.17 = \mathbf{60.83}$

16. **(D)**

    Plug in each set of values and determine if the inequality is true.
    $2(0) + 0 \leq -10$ FALSE
    $2(10) + 2 \leq -10$ FALSE
    $2(10) + 10 \leq -10$ FALSE

    $2(-10) + (-10) \leq -10$ **TRUE**

17. **(C)**

    $6(3^0) = 6(1) = \mathbf{6}$

18. **(D)**

    The sum of the internal angles of a quadrilateral is **360°**.

19. **(D)**

    Use FOIL to solve.
    $(3x + 2)(3x + 2) = 9x^2 + 6x + 6x + 4 = \mathbf{9x^2 + 12x + 4}$

20. **(D)**

    Use the volume to find the length of the cube's side.
    $V = s^3$
    $343 = s^3$
    $s = 7$ m
    Find the area of each side and multiply by 6 to find the total surface area.
    $7(7) = 49$ m
    $49(6) = \mathbf{294 \text{ m}^2}$

21. **(D)**

    Use the distance formula.
    $d = \sqrt{(x_2 - x_1)^2 + (y_2 - y_1)^2}$
    $= \sqrt{(-2 - 3)^2 + (-5 - 0)^2} = \sqrt{50} = \mathbf{5\sqrt{2}}$

22. **(A)**

    Substitute 8 for x and 2 for y in the expression.
    $3x + 7y - 4$
    $3(8) + 7(2) - 4 = 24 + 14 - 4 = \mathbf{34}$

23. **(B)**

    Use the Pythagorean theorem to determine which set of values forms a right triangle.
    $40^2 + 41^2 = 50^2$
    $3,281 \neq 2,500$
    $9^2 + 40^2 = 41^2$
    $\mathbf{1,681 = 1,681}$
    $9^2 + 30^2 = 40^2$
    $981 \neq 1,600$

$40^2 + 50^2 = 63^2$

$4{,}100 \neq 3{,}969$

24. (C)

Plug the given values into the equation and solve for t.

$d = v \times t$

$4{,}000 = 500 \times t$

$t = 8$ hours

25. (D)

Multiply the constants and add the exponents on each variable.

$3(6) = 18$

$x^2(x) = x^3$

$y(y^3) = y^4$

$z^4(z^2) = z^6$

$3x^2yz^4(6xy^3z^2) = \mathbf{18x^3y^4z^6}$

Electronics

1. **(C)**
   (A) is incorrect. The two charges are both negative and so will interact, causing them to move.
   (B) is incorrect. The charges are both negative, so they will repel, not attract, each other.
   (C) is correct. The two charges are both negative, so they will repel each other and move apart.
   (D) is incorrect. The two charges would move in the same direction only if they were being acted on by an outside force.

2. **(B)**
   (A) is incorrect. Ohms (Ω) is the unit for resistance.
   (B) is correct. Amperes (A) is the unit for current.
   (C) is incorrect. Volts (V) is the unit for voltage.
   (D) is incorrect. Coulombs (C) is the unit for charge.

3. **(B)**
   (A) is incorrect. There is a difference between conductors and insulators.
   (B) is correct. A conductor has free electrons that easily move current, while an insulator has restricted electrons that do not allow current to flow.
   (C) is incorrect. Electrons are not created or destroyed by electronics materials. (They can be created or destroyed in nuclear reactions, like in the sun.)
   (D) is incorrect. All materials will have heat created when electricity flows through them.

4. **(C)**
   (A) is incorrect. A fuse protects a circuit from high currents.
   (B) is incorrect. A power supply provides power to a circuit.
   (C) is correct. The ground is at zero potential and can ideally accept any amount of current.
   (D) is incorrect. A circuit breaker protects a circuit from high currents.

5. **(B)**
   (A) is incorrect. Current is not the same as heat.
   (B) is correct. The charge interactions and collisions that cause resistance also cause heat.
   (C) is incorrect. Heat is not created in this way.
   (D) is incorrect. Heat can lead to damage in electronic materials, so electronic designs usually minimize heat.

6. **(B)**
   Use Ohm's law.
   $V = IR = (0.001 \text{ A})(1000 \text{ }\Omega) = $ **1 V**

7. **(B)**
   Use the equation for finding power in a circuit.
   $P = IV = (0.85 \text{ A})(121 \text{ V}) = $ **102.9 W**

8. **(B)**
   (A) is incorrect. A transistor functions as a switch or amplifier.
   (B) is correct. A capacitor stores electrical charge.
   (C) is incorrect. A diode conducts electricity, usually in only one direction.
   (D) is incorrect. A rectifier converts an AC input to a DC input.

9. **(D)**
   Use the equation for equivalent resistance in a series circuit.
   $R_{eq} = R_1 + R_2 + ... + R_n$
   $R_{eq} = 1 \text{ k}\Omega + 2 \text{ k}\Omega + 0.5 \text{ k}\Omega = $ **3.5 kΩ**

10. **(B)**
    (A) is incorrect. The length of wire is measured in normal units of length: meters, centimeters, inches, etc.
    (B) is correct. The gauge is related to the diameter of the wire. Smaller gauge values are larger diameters. A larger diameter wire can carry more current.
    (C) is incorrect. The material composition of the wire determines the resistivity of the wire.
    (D) is incorrect. The cladding is an insulating material that keeps the wire protected.

11. **(D)**
    (A) is incorrect. The tree branch will connect the lines and create a short circuit.
    (B) is incorrect. The liquid will act as a conductor and create short circuits in the computer.
    (C) is incorrect. The wire will create a short circuit between the terminals of the battery.
    (D) is correct. If the computer is off, no current will flow and the electronics will most likely not be damaged. When the liquid dries, if there is no residue, the electronics should work again with no issues.

12. **(D)**
    (A) is incorrect. Neutrons have no charge and stay in place at the nuclei.
    (B) is incorrect. Protons have positive charge but do not move. They stay in place at the nuclei.
    (C) is incorrect. Electrons are the dominant charge carrier in N-type materials.
    (D) is correct. Holes (lack of electrons) are the dominant charge carrier in P-type materials.

13. **(A)**
    Use Ohm's law.
    $I = \frac{V}{R} = \frac{45\ V}{15\ \Omega} =$ **3 A**

14. **(A)**
    (A) is correct. The magnetic field always points from north to south poles.
    (B) is incorrect. The magnetic field always points from north to south poles.
    (C) is incorrect. East and west poles do not exist.
    (D) is incorrect. East and west poles do not exist.

15. **(C)**
    Set up a proportion to find the number of turns in the output coil.
    $$\frac{N_{output}}{N_{input}} = \frac{V_{output}}{V_{input}}$$
    $$N_{output} = (N_{input})\left(\frac{V_{output}}{V_{input}}\right)$$
    $$= (1{,}000\ \text{turns})\left(\frac{240\ V}{120\ V}\right)$$
    $N_{output} =$ **2,000 turns**

16. **(C)**
    (A) is incorrect. An alternator is an AC generator.
    (B) is incorrect. A rectifier converts AC to DC.
    (C) is correct. A dynamo is a DC generator.
    (D) is incorrect. An invertor converts DC to AC.

17. **(C)**
    (A) is incorrect. It is more complex than other motor types, so it is not cheaper to build.
    (B) is incorrect. Small torque and low speeds are not beneficial.
    (C) is correct. A compound motor benefits from a series motor (large starting torque) and shunt motor (good speed control).
    (D) is incorrect. The compound motor can operate at many different speeds.

18. **(C)**
    (A) is incorrect. The symbol for a voltmeter is:

    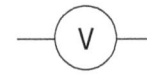

(B) is incorrect. The symbol for a cell is:

(C) is correct. This is the symbol for a capacitor.

(D) is incorrect. The symbol for a resistor is:

19. **(D)**

    Use Ohm's law.
    $V = IR = (10 \text{ A})(25 \text{ }\Omega) = \mathbf{250 \text{ V}}$

20. **(C)**

    (A) is incorrect. In a solid-state device, electricity flows through a semiconductor, not an insulator.

    (B) is incorrect. In a solid-state device, electricity flows through solid material, not a vacuum.

    (C) is correct. In a solid-state device, electricity flows through a semiconductor.

    (D) is incorrect. A transistor may be a solid-state device, but many other electrical components can also be solid-state devices.

Automotive and Shop Information

1. **(C)**
   (A) is incorrect. The control module monitors for spark.
   (B) is incorrect. The control module monitors the battery voltage.
   (C) is correct. The pick-up coil and reluctor are placed together. As the reluctor moves, the pick-up coil sends a signal to the control module.
   (D) is incorrect. The control module monitors the ignition coil.

2. **(C)**
   (A) is incorrect. Needle-nose pliers are designed for work on small components in small areas.
   (B) is incorrect. Adjustable joint pliers do not have the ability to cut.
   (C) is correct. Lineman pliers can cut and squeeze.
   (D) is incorrect. Locking pliers are used to lock onto objects and are not designed for small-area work.

3. **(D)**
   (A) is incorrect. The header pipes help direct exhaust gas to the catalytic converter.
   (B) is incorrect. EGR recirculates exhaust waste back to the engine.
   (C) is incorrect. The muffler quiets the exhaust.
   (D) is correct. Exhaust flows over the catalyst and a chemical reaction turns waste exhaust into cleaner exhaust.

4. **(A)**
   (A) is correct. A micrometer is designed to measure the outside diameter of shafts.
   (B) is incorrect. A micrometer cannot perform inside measurements.
   (C) is incorrect. A tape measure is used to measure boards.
   (D) is incorrect. Tension gauges measure spring tension.

5. **(A)**
   (A) is correct. A triangular file is used to remove material on internal surfaces.
   (B) is incorrect. A flat file is used to remove material on flat surfaces.
   (C) is incorrect. A rasp is used to remove large amounts of material on flat and curved surfaces.
   (D) is incorrect. Robertson screwdrivers are used to remove screws with square holes in the head.

6. **(C)**
   (A) is incorrect. The unibody is a load-bearing frame.
   (B) is incorrect. The floor and body are a one-piece design.
   (C) is correct. The unibody is a one-piece body design.
   (D) is incorrect. Stressed skin is a strong outer shell.

7. **(D)**
   (A) is incorrect. A circular saw is used for straight cuts.
   (B) is incorrect. These pliers are used to remove snap rings.
   (C) is incorrect. A miter saw is used for straight cuts at multiple angles.
   (D) is correct. A hole saw is used in combination with a drill to cut a circular hole in a board.

8. **(A)**
   (A) is correct. A CV joint connects to the transaxle. This is a flexible joint.
   (B) is incorrect. A universal joint normally will connect to a driveshaft.
   (C) is incorrect. A ball joint connects to the control arms.
   (D) is incorrect. A ball joint connects to control arms, and a universal joint normally connects to a driveshaft.

9. **(B)**
   (A) is incorrect. A Vernier caliper is used to measure.

(B) is correct. A roll-pin punch is designed to remove roll pins without damage.

(C) is incorrect. A center punch is too large to drive out a roll pin.

(D) is incorrect. A drift punch is used for alignment. Any other type of use would damage the pin.

10. **(A)**

   (A) is correct. Negative camber is the inward tilt of the wheel.

   (B) is incorrect. Positive camber is the outward tilt of the wheel.

   (C) is incorrect. Negative caster is the forward tilt of the wheel.

   (D) is incorrect. Positive caster is the rearward tilt of the wheel.

11. **(C)**

   (A) is incorrect. A Torx screwdriver works with screws that have a star hole in the head.

   (B) is incorrect. A Phillips screwdriver works with screws that have a cross slot in the head.

   (C) is correct. A Robertson screwdriver works with screws that have a square hole in the head.

   (D) is incorrect. A ratchet must be used with a Robertson socket.

12. **(D)**

   (A) is incorrect. The system is sealed. Once the fluid is filled and the cap is on, no fluid will escape.

   (B) is incorrect. If the system is dirty, the entire system should be flushed out and bled.

   (C) is incorrect. If there is air in the system, the pads will not grip properly.

   (D) is correct. Air in the system needs to be forced out by bleeding.

13. **(D)**

   (A) is incorrect. A tap is used to insert threads into a drilled hole.

   (B) is incorrect. A Vernier caliper takes inside and outside diameter measurements.

   (C) is incorrect. An inside caliper takes only inside diameter measurements.

   (D) is correct. A thread-pitch gauge is used to measure threads on a bolt.

14. **(B)**

   (A) is incorrect. The alternator charges the battery.

   (B) is correct. The rectifier changes AC to DC.

   (C) is incorrect. The battery supplies voltage to the alternator.

   (D) is incorrect. AC is supplied to the rectifier; DC is the output.

15. **(C)**

   (A) is incorrect. This wrench does not have jaws to adjust.

   (B) is incorrect. A combination wrench has a box on one end. The jaws are not adjustable on the other end.

   (C) is correct. The jaws of this wrench are adjusted with a thumbwheel.

   (D) is incorrect. The jaws of an open-end wrench are not adjustable.

16. **(C)**

   (A) is incorrect. An impact sensor detects when a crash has happened.

   (B) is incorrect. Piston knocking can be heard, but it is not detected by the sensor.

   (C) is correct. The knock sensor detects when detonation is happening. The sensor sends a signal for the ignition timing to adjust.

   (D) is incorrect. Emission sensors detect the state of the exhaust gases leaving the engine.

17. **(B)**

   (A) is incorrect. A ratchet and socket set is hand-powered and slower than an impact wrench and socket.

   (B) is correct. An impact wrench is pneumatic, or electrically driven, and is the best tool to quickly remove a nut or bolt.

(C) is incorrect. A combination wrench is hand-operated and cannot be used to remove a lug nut.

(D) is incorrect. A box-end wrench is hand-operated and cannot be used to remove a lug nut.

18. **(D)**

    (A) is incorrect. A wheel sensor sends a signal to the control module to activate the system.

    (B) is incorrect. A wheel sensor sends a signal to the control module to activate the system.

    (C) is incorrect. The LATCH system refers to anchored hardware points located in the rear passenger seats.

    (D) is correct. A light will notify the operator that tire pressure needs attention.

19. **(A)**

    (A) is correct. A claw hammer is designed to drive nails.

    (B) is incorrect. A rubber mallet is used for alignment operations.

    (C) is incorrect. A chuck and key are parts of a drill.

    (D) is incorrect. A hand drill is used for boring and turning operations.

20. **(A)**

    (A) is correct. The fuel injector injects fuel directly into the pre-combustion chamber (in indirect injection engines) or the combustion chamber (in direct injection engines), where ignition occurs.

    (B) is incorrect. There are no spark plugs in the pre-chamber or combustion chamber.

    (C) is incorrect. A spark plug is used in gasoline engines.

    (D) is incorrect. Indirect injection is only one process; many diesel engines use direct injection.

21. **(A)**

    (A) is correct. A ratchet in combination with a socket is used to remove bolts quickly in an open area.

(B) is incorrect. A combination wrench does not have a ratcheting action. This slows down removal.

(C) is incorrect. Using an open-end wrench in this case would likely round corners of the bolt head and would be a very slow process.

(D) is incorrect. There is no ratcheting action with a box-end wrench. This slows down removal.

22. **(A)**

    (A) is correct. These are undesirable emissions.

    (B) is incorrect. Carbon dioxide is emitted from the tailpipe.

    (C) is incorrect. Oxygen and carbon dioxide are emitted from the tailpipe.

    (D) is incorrect. These are emitted from the tailpipe.

23. **(A)**

    (A) is correct. Hand drills use keyless chucks for quick bit change.

    (B) is incorrect. A band saw does not have a chuck.

    (C) is incorrect. A nail gun does not have a chuck.

    (D) is incorrect. A drill press uses a chuck and key combination.

24. **(C)**

    (A) is incorrect. Air is needed for the vehicle to run properly, although the vehicle will adjust as needed.

    (B) is incorrect. Air is needed for the vehicle to run properly, although the vehicle will adjust as needed.

    (C) is correct. Cold air is heavier than hot air. More air means less fuel and a lean mixture.

    (D) is incorrect. Cold air is heavier than hot air.

25. **(D)**

    (A) is incorrect. A claw hammer is used for driving and pulling nails.

    (B) is incorrect. A rubber mallet is used for alignment of components without damage.

(C) is incorrect. This mallet is used in woodworking applications.

(D) is correct. A ball-peen hammer is used in metalworking applications.

Mechanical Comprehension

1. **(C)**
   Use Newton's second law to find the acceleration.
   $\Sigma F = ma = (1{,}000 \text{ kg})(10 \text{ m/s}^2) =$ **10,000 N**

2. **(C)**
   (A) is incorrect. A first-class lever has the fulcrum between the input and output forces, and the two forces point in opposite directions.
   (B) is incorrect. A second-class lever has the input and output on the same side of the fulcrum with the output force closer to the fulcrum than the input force.
   (C) is correct. A third-class lever has the input and output on the same side of the fulcrum with the input force closer to the fulcrum than the output force.
   (D) is incorrect. Fourth-class levers do not exist.

3. **(C)**
   (A) is incorrect. This is Newton's second law.
   (B) is incorrect. This is Newton's third law.
   (C) is correct. The net force is not always zero.
   (D) is incorrect. This is Newton's first law.

4. **(B)**
   Use the formula for power.
   $P = \left(\dfrac{\text{work done}}{\text{time}}\right)\left(\dfrac{100 \text{ J}}{10 \text{ s}}\right) =$ **10 W**

5. **(B)**
   Use the formula for mechanical advantage.
   $MA = \dfrac{F_{output}}{F_{input}} = \dfrac{4{,}000}{1{,}000} = \mathbf{4}$

6. **(B)**
   Find the new value of a using Newton's second law.
   $\Sigma F = ma$
   $a = \dfrac{\Sigma F}{m}$
   $a' = \dfrac{\Sigma F}{2m} = \dfrac{1}{2}\left(\dfrac{\Sigma F}{m}\right) = \dfrac{1}{2}(1 \text{ m/s}^2)$
   $= \mathbf{0.5 \text{ m/s}^2}$

7. **(D)**
   (A) is incorrect. Gravitation is a fundamental force.
   (B) is incorrect. Nuclear is a fundamental force.
   (C) is incorrect. Electromagnetic is a fundamental force.
   (D) is correct. Friction is not a fundamental force.

8. **(A)**
   (A) is correct. Friction is a force that opposes motion.
   (B) is incorrect. Friction is the result of two surfaces rubbing, not pushing, against each other.
   (C) is incorrect. This is called torque.
   (D) is incorrect. Friction increases with normal force.

9. **(A)**
   Sum the forces to find the net force on the mass.
   $\Sigma F = F - f_k = 100 \text{ N} - 90 \text{ N} = \mathbf{10 \text{ N}}$

10. **(B)**
    Use the formula for the mechanical advantage of a wheel and axle.
    $MA = \dfrac{r_{input}}{r_{output}} = \dfrac{0.1}{0.5} = \dfrac{1}{5}$

11. **(A)**
    (A) is correct. The normal force will be less than if the mass were on a horizontal plane. On a horizontal plane, all of the normal force is in the y-direction. On an inclined plane, the normal force is split into x- and y-components.
    (B) is incorrect. The opposite of this statement is true.
    (C) is incorrect. The normal force will change depending on the angle of the plane.

(D) is incorrect. The normal force exists regardless of the plane's angle.

12. **(C)**

    Multiply the liquid's density by its volume to find its mass.
    $m = \rho V = (100 \text{ kg/m}^3)(1 \text{ m}^3) = $ **100 kg**

13. **(B)**

    Use the formula for kinetic energy.
    $KE = \frac{1}{2}mv^2 = \frac{1}{2}(10 \text{ kg})(2 \text{ m/s})^2 = $ **20 J**

14. **(C)**

    Use the formula for acceleration.
    $a = \frac{(v_2 - v_1)}{t}$
    $a = \frac{(v_2 - 0)}{t}$
    $v_2 = at = 9.8 \text{ m/s}^2 \cdot 1 \text{ s} = $ **9.8 m/s**

15. **(A)**

    (A) is correct. Friction will convert mechanical energy into heat.
    (B) is incorrect. Potential energy does not generate heat.
    (C) is incorrect. Work energy does not create heat.
    (D) is incorrect. Gravity does not generate heat.

16. **(A)**

    Wood chips will compress, which increases the time that a force is applied during a collision. The force experienced by a slowing object will be smaller if the time is increased. The other three material would not compress and thus would not increase the time of impact.

17. **(C)**

    Momentum within a system is conserved, so the system will have the same momentum before and after the collision. The system's final momentum will be **200 kg m/s**.

18. **(A)**

    (A) is correct. According to Newton's third law, the normal force will be equal and opposite of the person's weight.
    (B) is incorrect. While the magnitude of the force is correct, the direction is not; it should be opposite of the person's weight (toward the person from the floor).
    (C) is incorrect. While the direction of the force is correct, the magnitude is not; it should equal the person's weight (300 N).
    (D) is incorrect. Neither the magnitude of the force nor its direction is correct.

19. **(D)**

    Use the formula for mechanical advantage in a screw.
    $MA = \frac{2\pi r}{h} = \frac{2\pi(0.5 \text{ in})}{0.25 \text{ in}} = $ **4π**

20. **(C)**

    Use Newton's second law to find the acceleration of the charge.
    $\Sigma F = ma$
    $20 \text{ N} = (10 \text{ kg})(a)$
    $a = 2 \text{ m/s}^2$

21. **(D)**

    Use the formula for displacement.
    $\Delta x = vt = (40 \text{ m/s})(2 \text{ s}) = $ **80 m**

22. **(A)**

    (A) is correct. When the man pushes on the rock, static friction points opposite the direction of the applied force with the same magnitude.
    (B) is incorrect. Gravity pulls the rock towards the Earth, but it does not counteract the horizontal force being applied by the man.
    (C) is incorrect. The normal force pushes up on the rock. It does not counteract the horizontal force being applied by the man.
    (D) is incorrect. The buoyant force only occurs when an object is floating or submerged in a liquid.

23. **(A)**

    (A) is correct. Tension is created by hanging objects, so a box sliding

down a ramp will not experience any tension.
(B) is incorrect. Gravity pulls the box down the ramp.
(C) is incorrect. Friction oppose the force of gravity that is pulling the box down the ramp.
(D) is incorrect. The normal force will be perpendicular to the surface of the incline.

24. **(A)**
Find the ratio of the number of output teeth to the number of input teeth.
$$\text{gear ratio} = \frac{N_{output}}{N_{input}} = \frac{3,500}{1,000} = \mathbf{3.5}$$

25. **(A)**
Use the formula for torque.
$\tau = rF = (0.5 \text{ m})(4 \text{ N}) = \mathbf{2 \text{ Nm}}$

Assembling Objects

1. (C)
2. (D)
3. (D)
4. (C)
5. (D)
6. (B)
7. (B)
8. (C)
9. (A)
10. (A)
11. (B)
12. (D)
13. (A)
14. (D)
15. (D)
16. (D)
17. (A)
18. (D)
19. (B)
20. (A)
21. (D)
22. (A)
23. (C)
24. (A)
25. (B)

Milton Keynes UK
Ingram Content Group UK Ltd.
UKHW030613140224
437800UK00003B/39